Susan B. Anthony: Echoes of a Revolutionary Legacy

MARKO D

ISBN:9798862655810

Table of Contents

Acknowledgments

Who walks a path without a guide or sails a sea without a compass? Our journey through the life of Susan B. Anthony is much the same. Before delving deeper, we must pause to acknowledge those who lit the path and helped paint a fuller, richer portrait of this formidable figure.

Firstly, a heartfelt nod to the numerous historians and scholars whose tireless efforts in archives and libraries, both digital and dusty, have gifted us the raw material from which Susan's story is woven. Without them, would we really grasp the magnitude of her impact or the intensity of her convictions?

To the educators: those passionate professors and high school history teachers who have kept Susan's spirit alive in classrooms nationwide. You've recounted facts and instilled a sense of wonder, leading countless to ask: How did one woman challenge the status quo so fiercely? And how can I, too, make a difference?

Of course, Susan's narrative isn't just built upon the giants of academia. The personal anecdotes, the handed-down family tales, and the community legends add the color and nuance we so desperately need to see her as more than just an icon – but as a living, breathing entity. Thank you to those who've shared these snippets, whether through interviews, letters, or over a cup of steaming coffee. Your stories have been invaluable.

One can only speak of Susan B. Anthony by mentioning her contemporaries. Elizabeth Cady Stanton, you've been more than just a co-worker in the suffrage movement. In letters and journals, your reflections mirror Susan's soul, showcasing the depth of your mutual respect and camaraderie.

To the Anthony family, for preserving her letters and diaries and ensuring that her legacy is not just in what she did but in her words and thoughts. In them, we find the very essence of Susan: passionate, determined, and unyielding.

Lastly, dear reader, a nod to you. By seeking to understand Susan B. Anthony, you're not just learning about history – you're actively participating in the continuing dialogue about equality, justice, and the kind of world we wish to craft for future generations. So, let's embark on this journey together, and may you find inspiration on every page.

Let us now turn the pages and immerse ourselves in the world of Susan B. Anthony, where every challenge faced is a lesson and every triumph a beacon for us all...

Why Susan B. Anthony Matters Today

In a world that seems hurtling forward at lightning speed, why should we pause, look back, and fixate our attention on a woman who lived well over a century ago? The answer is simple: Susan B. Anthony's story is not confined to the dusty pages of history. It's alive, vibrant, and eerily relevant even today.

Picture this: you're flipping through a modern magazine, and an article on gender equality catches your eye. As you read about ongoing battles for equal pay, representation, and rights, does it ever cross your mind that these modern struggles are grounded in the legacies of pioneers like Susan? Without her, would we even be having these conversations today?

Anthony wasn't just a woman with a mission; she was the mission. In a society that had predefined roles for its women, Susan was a square peg in a round hole. Refusing to be confined, she reshaped the very hole itself. Now, isn't that the hallmark of a visionary?

From the tender age of 17, Anthony's journey began. The world told her, "This is how things are." But she responded, "But what if they could be different?" And different she made them. From challenging educational norms for women to asserting their right to vote, her life was a series of rebellions, each more audacious than the last.

Yet, it wasn't a solo journey. Collaborating with Elizabeth Cady Stanton, Lucy Stone, and other stalwarts of her time, Anthony laid down the foundations of movements that would reverberate for centuries. But why? Why did she pour her very essence into these causes? Simple: Susan B. Anthony saw the next day. She envisioned a world where her nieces, grandnieces, and countless women unknown to her could live with dignity, voice, and choice.

So, when we cast our votes today, voice our opinions, or walk with our heads held a little higher, we're walking in the shadows of giants like Anthony. And that's precisely why she matters, not as a relic of the past but as a beacon for the future.

What would Susan say if she saw our world today? Would she be proud of the progress or urge us to push even harder? One can only speculate. But this much is clear: in every step toward gender equality, in every voice that refuses to be silenced, Susan B. Anthony lives on.

So, the next time you think of Susan, don't just remember her. Celebrate her. In understanding her story, we find the strength and inspiration to write our own...

Chapter 1

The Birth of a Revolutionary

Imagine a time when women, by their gender, were consigned to the shadows. Picture a world not too distant from today, where the voices of half the population were stifled. But amidst that hush, a cry emerged. It wasn't just any cry: it was the voice of Susan B. Anthony, a woman destined to shake the very foundations of society.

Susan's story begins on February 15, 1820, in a quaint Massachusetts town. Adams, where rolling hills met tight-knit communities, witnessed the dawn of a life that would forever change its course. As the second eldest of seven, Susan's upbringing was nestled in the Quaker tradition: a faith rooted in equality and justice. Could this early exposure forge the fiery advocate we came to know?

Daniel Anthony, Susan's father, was a man of firm convictions. A stern cotton manufacturer, he championed temperance and anti-slavery movements. Yet, behind that exterior, he held a unique belief for his time: an unwavering faith in his daughter's abilities. Lucelia, Guelma, and Susan weren't just named in the family ledger. To Daniel, they represented potential waiting to unfurl.

It wasn't merely her father's influence that stirred young Susan. Hannah Anthony, her mother, was a pillar of grace and resilience. Susan learned the delicate dance of compassion intertwined with an indomitable spirit from her. Observing the world around her, Susan couldn't help but ask: Why were women relegated to the backdrop? Why couldn't they hold the same positions, bear the same responsibilities, and voice the same opinions as men?

Schooling for Susan was an ever-evolving affair. Initially schooled in her hometown, she soon moved to a Philadelphia boarding school. However, financial hardships led to a return home, where her educational journey took an unconventional twist. Under her father's guidance, she dove into math and science. Why? Because to Daniel, gender was no barrier to brilliance.

But knowledge alone wasn't enough for Susan. She yearned to apply it, to carve a niche in the world where her voice mattered. As a young woman, she found herself as a teacher. While she was molding young minds, life was, in turn, shaping her. The schoolyard was where Susan recognized the first wage disparities between men and women. Such discrepancies posed questions: Why the difference? Isn't labor's value universal, regardless of who performs it?

Kindled by personal experiences and fanned by societal injustices, this spark gave birth to the revolution we honor today. This wasn't just a journey of a woman striving for her place. It was the inception of a movement, a call for equality, and a beacon for all those who felt unheard.

But remember, before she was a revolutionary, she was Susan from Adams, Massachusetts. Could anyone have foreseen the powerhouse she would become from such humble beginnings? As we peel back the layers of her life, we realize revolutions don't just happen. They're born out of moments, choices, and, sometimes, from the quiet corners of Adams...

Early Beginnings: Adams, Massachusetts

In the embrace of Adams, Massachusetts, a tapestry of historical threads intertwines. It's a place where the whispers of the past meld with the murmurs of the present. Yet, among those many voices, one stands out, echoing louder, demanding our attention. Who? None other than Susan B. Anthony.

The Anthony household in Adams wasn't just any home. It was a crucible where ideas fermented and beliefs took root. Can you picture it? A sturdy New England home, with the cold winds outside shaping its character, just as the ideas within molded a young Susan. Born in 1820, she was not initially destined for greatness, but the very air of Adams seemed to conspire to make her so.

You see, Adams had this unique blend: an atmosphere of rigorous intellectual debate paired with the raw authenticity of frontier life. And it's in this milieu that Susan's parents, Daniel and Hannah, raised their daughter. They were not just Quakers but thinkers. Believers in justice advocate for freedom. Does it surprise you then that their beliefs seeped into Susan's very being?

Imagine a young Susan, eyes wide with curiosity, sitting at their dining table. The flicker of candlelight dances on her face as she listens intently to discussions about abolition, temperance, and - dare we say it - women's rights. These weren't just debates; they were the lifeblood of the Anthony family. Susan wasn't merely an observer. No, she was a participant. Her father, Daniel, never saw her as just another child. He saw potential: a bright, curious mind ready to question and challenge.

Schooling? It was a patchwork of experiences for Susan. First, a district school in Adams, and later, a boarding school in Philadelphia. But the true lessons? They were learned at home. When the family faced financial hardships, Susan returned to Adams. She threw herself into self-education, consuming books and engaging in hearty discussions. Those formative years in Adams were instrumental. It was not about formal education but about a mindset, an ethos.

And let's remember the influence of her mother, Hannah. A woman of grace, she instilled in her daughter the virtues of compassion and resilience. From Hannah, Susan learned to balance strength with empathy, to fight, yes, but also to understand. Hannah's lessons were invaluable, teaching her daughter that it's not just about raising your voice; it's about making sure it speaks for those unheard.

With its rolling hills and spirited debates, Adams wasn't just a backdrop for Susan B. Anthony's life. It was the stage upon which her beliefs were forged, and her passions ignited. With its tight-knit community and unyielding New England spirit, that town played an unsung role in shaping one of history's most iconic advocates for women's rights.

So, the next time you think of Susan B. Anthony, remember Adams, Massachusetts. For it's there, among its quaint streets and storied homes, that a legend was born. And if you listen closely enough, you might still hear the echoes of a young girl's dreams that would change a nation.

The Anthonys' Quaker Beliefs

In the gentle heartland of Massachusetts, where Susan B. Anthony's story began, another tale interwoven with hers: that of the Quaker Anthonys. Now, one might ask, why dive deep into the family's religious convictions? Because, dear reader, understanding the Anthonys' Quaker beliefs isn't just about understanding a religion; it's about grasping the very fabric that clothed Susan's spirit and ambition.

The Quakers, or the Society of Friends, held revolutionary tenets for the era. Equality. Simplicity. Peace. Integrity. These weren't just words; they were guiding principles. For the Anthony family, these beliefs manifested in their worship and daily life. And how could they not? Living in a world rife with injustice, the Anthonys held fast to a faith that believed in the innate light within every individual.

Daniel and Hannah, Susan's parents, were the pillars of this devout home. Daniel, ever the intellectual, championed the importance of reason and discourse. Through his eyes, Susan saw a world where beliefs were not just recited but deeply pondered upon. And Hannah? She was the beating heart, teaching her children the art of compassion and resilience. Their Quaker values meant that everyone, regardless of gender or race, deserved respect and love. What a radical thought in a world that often preached otherwise!

The Anthony household, thus, was one of discussion and debate. Imagine the setting: the rustic living room, dimly lit, with family members passionately discussing issues of the day. Slavery. Women's rights. Temperance. Is it unusual for a young girl to be a part of such dialogues? But in the Anthony home, Susan wasn't an outsider. Thanks to the Quaker belief in equality, she was right there, in the thick of things, absorbing, learning, and voicing her opinions.

It's no exaggeration to say that these Quaker ideals shaped Susan B. Anthony's lifelong pursuits. The idea that everyone had an "inner light," a divine essence, resonated deeply with her. This belief propelled her to champion those silenced by society. It wasn't just about women's suffrage but human rights. How could one stand by when their faith taught that every soul had value?

Moreover, the Quaker emphasis on simplicity and authenticity became the backbone of Susan's own life. She didn't desire accolades or grandeur. Instead, she was fueled by a genuine desire to make a difference, to live a life that mirrored her convictions.

And it was this upbringing, steeped in Quakerism, that gave Susan the audacity to dream big. To challenge norms. To stand firm in the face of adversity. The Anthonys' Quaker beliefs weren't just doctrines; they were a call to action, a plea to make the world better.

So, don't just see the reformer when you think of Susan B. Anthony. See the Quaker child, nurtured in a home where faith was alive, vibrant, and challenging. See the woman whose family ties weren't just about blood but a shared belief in the potential for good in everyone. And remember: it's often in the quiet convictions of the heart where revolutions are born.

Early Experiences of Injustice

What's that whispering voice, that gentle nudge within the depths of a person's soul, urging them to take a stand? For many, it remains dormant, silenced by life's conveniences or fears. But for Susan B. Anthony, that whisper was more like a roar from her earliest days, propelling her into a life of tireless activism. The seed? A series of early experiences acquainted her with the bitter taste of injustice.

Imagine being a young Susan in the 1830s. The world outside is full of opportunities. But wait! There's a catch. Those opportunities are meant for some. Susan faced her first glaring confrontation with inequality in a district school in Battenville, New York. She pondered why the boys were enjoying lessons in the long division. At the same time, she and her fellow female students were left to grapple with simple arithmetic? The realization hit her with a profound sense of inequity: her education was being stunted, not because of a lack of capability, but solely because of her gender.

Yet, the indignities didn't stop at the schoolhouse door. Young Anthony observed the tight chains binding women everywhere: in economic spheres, political arenas, and even within the very sanctum of their homes. Witnessing her mother, a woman of immense strength and character, having no legal rights to the family's property or even her own earnings made Susan wonder. How could society, which preached values of freedom and justice, uphold such blatant double standards?

The Anthony home was, however, not a place of passive acceptance. The echo of Quaker beliefs, emphasizing equality, reverberated within its walls. Discussions around the hearth centered on issues of the day, like the abolition of slavery and temperance. Fueled by passion and a shared quest for justice, these talks molded Susan's perspectives. What if she thought she could bridge the gap between these discussions and real-world change?

The most defining incident of young Susan's life was her family's financial ruin during the Panic of 1837. The Anthony family, once financially secure, was reduced to near poverty. Experiencing firsthand the vulnerabilities of economic instability, especially for women, Susan's drive for reform took on a more emotional edge.

The world told her women to be passive and accept their lot with grace and silence. But Susan, with a spirit as indomitable as the roaring Niagara, refused to be boxed in. Each act of discrimination, every whispered doubt about a woman's worth, only added fuel to her fire.

Did she ever doubt, even for a moment, the path she'd chosen? Perhaps. But Susan's early encounters with injustice fortified her resolve. They became the tales she would recount, the lessons she'd use to educate, and the foundation upon which she built her legacy of activism.

So, next time you come across the name "Susan B. Anthony," remember the young girl whose spirit was ignited by dreams of a brighter future and the sharp pangs of injustice she felt in her formative years. And let's ask ourselves: what whispers or roars are we hearing today? And what are we going to do about them?

Chapter 2

Education and Abolition

Have you ever wondered what fuels the fire in the belly of trailblazers? For Susan B. Anthony, two pivotal facets of her early years fanned the flames of her passion – her thirst for education and her fierce belief in abolition.

Picture a young Susan. As a daughter in the Quaker household of Daniel and Lucy Read Anthony, she grew up in a world where the conventional expectations for women were clear and limiting. Yet, the Anthony home was different. In there, ideas swirled, minds questioned, and young Susan imbibed values of equality and education. The Quaker belief in gender equality wasn't just theoretical in the Anthony household. It was practiced, felt, and lived.

Education became Susan's first battleground. While many dismissed the idea of women getting a formal education, Anthony challenged this notion. Why should the doors of knowledge be barred for half the human race? Does not every mind, regardless of gender, yearn for enlightenment? The limited educational opportunities available to her only heightened her awareness of the inequities women faced. And it was here, in education, that Anthony's advocacy began its steady hum, which would soon turn into a roar.

Parallel to her advocacy for women's education was her involvement in the abolitionist movement. And if you're thinking, "What was the connection?" the answer lies in the word 'equality.' The same principle that led her to question gender roles led her to challenge and condemn racial discrimination. The horror of slavery, a blot on the fabric of a nation that proclaimed liberty, was impossible for Anthony to ignore.

Joining forces with Frederick Douglass, a formerly enslaved person and close family friend, Anthony threw herself into the abolitionist cause with the same enthusiasm as her push for women's rights. Their collaborations were legendary: Douglass brought firsthand accounts of the horrors of slavery, and Anthony, with her powerful rhetoric, helped amplify the message. Together, they painted a picture of a world where freedom was the birthright of every individual, irrespective of race or gender.

Now, can you see it? Can you see how Susan's early experiences with education and abolition intertwined, creating a tapestry of activism? It's as if the universe itself was aligning circumstances, forging a path for Anthony to emerge as one of history's most stalwart champions of rights.

The roots of Anthony's activism were watered by her early brushes with education inequities and fortified by her stand against racial prejudice. These were not merely causes she fought for but parts of a singular vision. A vision of a world without chains, be they chains of ignorance or bondage.

And so, as we journey through her life, remember: it was in the classrooms and anti-slavery gatherings of her youth that the seeds of Susan B. Anthony's legendary advocacy were first sown...

Teaching and Early Learnings

Imagine, if you will, a classroom from the mid-19th century. Rustic wooden desks, chalk dust in the air, and students with rosy cheeks and curious eyes. At the helm stands a young woman, vibrant and animated. That woman? None other than Susan B. Anthony.

The classroom was Anthony's initial stage, long before the broader American landscape became her platform for advocacy. But what drew her into teaching? And how did those early days mold the icon we recognize today?

The Anthony family valued education. For them, a well-educated mind wasn't just an asset but an obligation. Naturally, Susan was encouraged to pursue learning, and this encouragement eventually led her to step into the role of a teacher. Yet, teaching was about more than just transmitting knowledge. For Anthony, it was more about igniting passion. Can you envision her captivating her students with lessons that were far more than rote memorization, instilling values of equality and justice in them?

However, the classroom also served as a mirror to the disparities of the time. Susan was paid a fraction of what her male counterparts earned. Fair? Certainly not. But it was the status quo. Here, amidst lesson plans and student queries, Anthony's consciousness about gender inequality intensified. Why should she, with the same enthusiasm and dedication, earn any less? The reality of this wage disparity stung, but it also fueled.

Beyond the paycheck, the classroom also offered glimpses into the societal expectations of women. Girls were expected to be demure to focus on "feminine" subjects. Susan, however, had a different plan. She encouraged her female students to think, question, and aspire beyond the confined roles society had outlined for them. Is it possible that some of the early seeds for her later advocacy for women's rights were sown right there, among chalkboards and eager young minds?

Her teaching journey spanned well over a decade, but as with all things, chapters end. Susan B. Anthony transitioned from the classroom, but the lessons she learned there? They were indelible. The classroom was her first tryst with leadership, her first taste of gender biases, and, most importantly, her initial realization that change was not just necessary but imperative.

So, when we think of Susan B. Anthony, while it's easy to recall her monumental speeches and tireless advocacy, let's remember the classroom. There, amidst young learners, the educator became the student, learning firsthand about the battles she would later dedicate her life to fighting.

Meeting Frederick Douglass

Imagine two powerhouses, both champions of human rights, standing in a room. Sparks of change fly as ideas intertwine and plans for action form. This isn't a fictional meeting of minds but a moment in history when Susan B. Anthony met Frederick Douglass.

The backdrop: Rochester, New York. Anthony's own hometown had become a hotbed for progressive thinking. With the air thick with conversations of rights and freedom, was it fate or mere chance that brought these two trailblazers together? Whatever it was, it irrevocably changed both of their lives.

Now, Frederick Douglass: an escaped enslaved person turned prominent abolitionist. His journey from chains to a free voice, ringing out against the ills of slavery, resonated far and wide. You're not far off if you're picturing a man of fierce determination and undeniable eloquence. And Susan? While she may have initially been recognized as an advocate for women's rights, her heart throbbed with the universal rhythm of equality for all.

So, when these two met, what emerged wasn't just a friendship but a symbiotic advocacy partnership. Together, they recognized that the fight for black rights and women's rights weren't distinct battles but intertwined struggles in pursuing universal suffrage.

Still, let's be honest: it wasn't all sunshine and rainbows. Their collaboration saw its fair share of disagreements. For instance, after the Civil War, the question arose: should the push for black men's voting rights take precedence over the universal suffrage movement? Tensions simmered, and at times, the two clashed. Douglass, mindful of the hostile South, believed in prioritizing voting rights for black men.

Understanding this urgency, Anthony couldn't help but question: when would it be the woman's turn?

Yet, isn't it true that the fiercest of friendships often weather the harshest storms? Their disagreements, although profound, never diminished their mutual respect. The shared vision of a world where every human, irrespective of race or gender, had a voice was too potent, too vital.

It's worth noting that their alliance was open to more than just conference rooms and public speeches. They celebrated personal milestones, with Anthony attending Douglass's last marriage and Douglass, in turn, giving a touching eulogy at Anthony's funeral. This mutual admiration society wasn't just about shared goals and a shared journey of pushing boundaries and challenging societal norms.

Picture this: Anthony, standing beside Douglass on a platform, speaking to a sea of faces, many hostile, others curious, and a few supportive. The energy between them was palpable. Their words? A clarion call for change.

When we think of Susan B. Anthony's legacy, it's essential to remember that she didn't walk her path alone. By her side, at many pivotal moments, stood Frederick Douglass. Together, they epitomized the power of collaboration in advocacy, teaching us a timeless lesson about unity, resilience, and the relentless pursuit of justice.

The Temperance Movement

Can you imagine when alcohol held such sway over society that it sparked a nationwide movement for its prohibition? It might sound almost dystopian but delve into 19th-century America, and you'll find just that. At the heart of it stood Susan B. Anthony, a titan of activism. And while her name is more commonly linked with women's suffrage, the Temperance Movement first kindled her fiery spirit for social change.

The temperance crusade didn't merely spring out of nowhere. The fabric of society then was deeply marred by excessive alcohol consumption. Picture this: families torn apart, livelihoods lost, and communities devastated by the vice-like grip of alcoholism. Sounds tragic.

Now, why was it that women, in particular, took up the mantle against this societal ill? The truth lies in the home. Women bore the brunt of their husbands' drunkenness, facing domestic abuse, financial hardship, and societal shame. With their family lives in turmoil, women had a clear stake in this fight: the desire for safe homes and stable families.

Enter Susan B. Anthony. A young teacher in New York, Anthony saw firsthand the destruction alcohol wrought on society. The tales she'd heard, the scenes she'd witnessed: men squandering their earnings at taverns, leaving their families in dire straits, children suffering at the hands of intoxicated parents. How could she, or anyone, stand by and watch?

With Elizabeth Cady Stanton, another formidable force for change, Anthony leaped into the temperance arena. They believed that if women had a political voice, they could drive legislative change against the alcohol menace. Simple reasoning. Give women the vote, and they'll protect their homes.

However, their involvement in the Temperance Movement could have been smoother sailing. In 1853, during a state temperance convention, Anthony's attempt to speak was rebuffed simply because she was a woman. Picture the irony: she was deemed fit enough to rally behind the cause but not to voice her opinions! This snub only deepened her resolve. It wasn't just about alcohol anymore; it was about a woman's place in society and her right to be heard.

While the movement did gather momentum, leading to the eventual Prohibition era in the 1920s, Anthony's involvement was transformative in more ways than one. Her experiences within the temperance circles became a stepping stone to championing broader women's rights. The linkages she saw – between alcohol abuse, women's suffrage, and domestic tranquility – underscored a deeper truth: the personal is political.

In retrospect, the Temperance Movement was not just about curbing alcohol consumption. It was a backdrop against which women's societal roles were redefined and reshaped. This period saw women transition from silent homemakers to vocal change-makers. In that transformative journey, Susan B. Anthony etched her name as a temperance advocate and a beacon for women's rights and social justice. What a journey, indeed!

Chapter 3

The Anthony-Stanton Partnership

Have you ever pondered the magic that occurs when two distinct minds align, propelled by a common cause? It's an alchemical reaction transcending the ordinary. And within the sprawling tapestry of American history, few partnerships shimmer as luminously as that of Susan B. Anthony and Elizabeth Cady Stanton.

Theirs wasn't a casual meeting of minds. No, it was a force of nature, a confluence of shared passion and purpose. So how did these two women, each powerful in her own right, become such a formidable pair?

The stage was set in 1851. Engrossed in her fight for women's rights, Stanton met Anthony through a mutual acquaintance. From that first meeting, it became evident: here were two women whose ideals, though rooted in the same soil of justice, sprouted in complementary directions. Anthony's unyielding organizational skills and indomitable spirit combined with Stanton's flair for rhetoric and deep-seated intellectualism. Like puzzle pieces, they fit.

Imagine their countless nights strategizing, their fervent discussions illuminating the room. Could they have known the monumental shifts their union would usher in? Stanton, primarily stationed at home due to familial obligations, often crafted compelling speeches and writings. Anthony? She became the voice that carried those words, reaching corners of the nation Stanton couldn't.

Yet, even the most iconic partnerships always have their challenges. Theirs faced criticism from all corners. Some said Stanton's ideas were too radical; others thought Anthony too confrontational. And yes, they had their disagreements, their moments of tension. But isn't that the mark of a genuine partnership? The ability to weather storms, hand in hand, eyes set on the horizon of change.

The duo remained a beacon of hope through the suffrage movement's trials and tribulations. Their combined efforts gave birth to *The Revolution*, a groundbreaking newspaper that loudly and proudly championed women's rights. And though, as with any venture, there were highs and lows, successes and setbacks, the Anthony-Stanton partnership stood unwavering.

The letters they exchanged reveal so much: mutual respect, admiration, even moments of levity amidst the most challenging times. They celebrated each other's victories, offered solace during defeats, and consistently pushed the envelope, challenging societal norms and each other.

To reduce their relationship to mere collaboration would be an injustice. This was a sisterhood. Beyond the public eye, beyond the rallies and speeches, they shared moments of profound personal connection. Births, deaths, joys, sorrows - life's messy glory.

As we look back, the impact of the Anthony-Stanton duo on the American landscape is undeniable. Their legacy, built on mutual trust and unwavering commitment to the cause, serves as a beacon for all who dream of a better world. And if there's one takeaway from their story, it's this: when spirited souls join forces, history doesn't stand a chance.

Elizabeth Cady Stanton

If you will, picture a world where society was sculpted in layers: men at the top and women, well, somewhere below. Not quite a canvas of equality. Two spirited women felt an irrepressible urge to rewrite the narrative in such a world. And their paths converged in a meeting so fateful that the threads of history tugged and adjusted themselves. This was the day Susan B. Anthony met Elizabeth Cady Stanton.

1851, Seneca Falls. Who would've guessed that a casual introduction on a bustling street would lead to a partnership so powerful? Their personalities were akin to fire and water. Stanton, the fountainhead of revolutionary ideas, and Anthony, the unstoppable force ensuring those ideas took root in the world. Two sides of the same coin, flipping endlessly in tandem, each necessary for the other.

What was it that connected them so profoundly? Was it a shared vision? A common frustration with society's shackles? Anthony had heard whispers of Stanton's impassioned speeches, her calls for women to reclaim their rightful places as equals. And Stanton? She knew of Anthony's ceaseless efforts and her tenacity in campaigning for change. But when they met, they realized they weren't just looking at an ally; they were looking at a mirror reflecting their own determination.

The bond was almost instant. Stanton would often be the pen, crafting compelling arguments with eloquence. On the other hand, Anthony was the voice, bringing those words to the masses, igniting minds and hearts. Their rhythm was palpable. One would spark an idea, and the other would fan it into a roaring blaze.

The partnership was with its bumps. Differences in opinion? Naturally, they had them. But remember, disagreement is often the crucible where the most transformative ideas are forged. Stanton's sometimes radical perspectives found balance in Anthony's methodical approach. Together, they navigated the tricky terrain of social reform, pulling each other up, challenging norms, and questioning the unquestionable.

Why did this partnership thrive in a world teetering on skepticism and doubt? Trust. At its core, their relationship was a testament to the power of trust. Trust in each other's abilities, their shared mission, and, most importantly, the belief that the world could change one step at a time.

The resonance of their alliance echoed far and wide. The women's suffrage movement gained momentum, buoyed by their combined energies. Journals, speeches, conventions: their influence was everywhere, shaping, nudging, and sometimes shaking the collective consciousness.

In our quest to understand the tapestry of history, it's essential to recognize moments that aren't just about dates and events. It's about connections. And the day Susan B. Anthony locked eyes with Elizabeth Cady Stanton, history didn't just witness a meeting; it felt a tremor. Because when like-minded souls come together, the world doesn't stand still; it shifts. And shift it did!

Strategies and Campaigns

Imagine a world amid change. Rumbles of progress echo in the distance, but resistance is fierce. Susan B. Anthony stood as an unwavering beacon at the heart of this shifting terrain. What was her secret sauce? One word: Strategy. But strategy isn't a solitary endeavor. It thrives on collaboration and the melding of complementary strengths. This was the essence of Anthony's campaigns.

How does one spark a revolution? Susan knew it wasn't by repeatedly beating on the same door. It was about finding that hidden window, slightly ajar, and pushing it wide open. Her strategies were a mix of innovation and sheer grit. A protest here, a thought-provoking speech there, petitions, and boots-on-the-ground activism. But behind each of these actions lay a well-thought-out plan.

Anthony wasn't just a participant in her campaigns; she was the maestro. The meticulous organization of events, the careful crafting of messaging, the selection of venues, the allies chose. Every decision was part of a grand design. In all these endeavors, one consistent presence was Elizabeth Cady Stanton. Their collaboration was legendary, but have you ever stopped to wonder why? Why did these two personalities mesh so well together?

Stanton was a powerhouse of ideas. Her mind was a swirling vortex of concepts, blueprints, and radical thoughts. But for a vision to become a reality, it needs grounding. That's where Anthony shone. She took Stanton's ideas, refined them, and laid out a clear roadmap. It was as if Stanton sketched the dream, and Anthony provided the bricks and mortar to build it. Together, they were a force of nature: the dreamer and the doer.

Did they always agree? No, they did not. Disagreements, differences in approach, and moments of frustration were as much a part of their collaboration as their successes. But here's the fascinating part. These differences didn't pull them apart; they added depth to their strategies. Stanton would sometimes aim for the stars, and Anthony, ever the pragmatist, would find ways to build the ladder to reach them.

One of their most iconic campaigns was the push for women's right to vote. At the time, even uttering such an idea was blasphemous. But this duo was still possible. They used every tool: publishing rights journals, organizing conventions, and relentless lobbying. And at every step, they ensured their strategies were rooted in their complementary strengths.

Imagine a convention. Stanton would enthrall the audience with her eloquence, making them visualize a world where women stood as equals. As the applause died, Anthony would step in, providing clear steps to turn that vision into reality, rallying the troops and mobilizing action. This was their magic: painting a picture and then providing the palette to bring it to life.

In the annals of history, few partnerships rival the synergy between Susan B. Anthony and Elizabeth Cady Stanton. Their distinct yet complementary strengths wove a tapestry of campaigns and strategies that not only defined their era but also lit the way for generations to come. They teach us a powerful lesson: true strength lies in having a vision and crafting the path to realize it. And when two minds, so aligned in purpose yet diverse in approach, come together, the world better watch out!

Disagreements and Resolve

Have you ever been so certain of a path, only to find a close ally sees things from a completely different perspective? It can be maddening. But disagreements, when navigated with grace and determination, can be the crucible in which ideas are honed and refined. Susan B. Anthony knew this dance all too well.

Susan and her closest collaborator, Elizabeth Cady Stanton, were a dynamic duo. Their strengths interwove seamlessly, creating a fabric of activism that, to many, seemed unbreakable. But let's delve deeper. Everything was in harmony and accord behind the scenes. Well, life's tapestry is rarely woven with a single thread.

With her expansive mind and audacious visions, Stanton often sought drastic societal shifts. She envisioned a world dramatically different from the present, where women didn't just vote but held the reins of power. This world had no ceilings, glass or otherwise. Exciting. But with radical vision comes potential pitfalls.

Here, Anthony, with her pragmatic nature, would step in. She recognized the merits of Stanton's views but was acutely aware of the societal pulse. The world was not ready for some of Stanton's ideas. Susan believed in incremental victories. Why? Because every small win was a step towards their shared dream. But imagine the tension. How do you tell a close friend that their vision might be too grand for the current times?

Disagreements arose naturally. Heated debates filled their meetings, with both women staunchly defending their positions. Some of these disagreements seemed to be the end of a potent partnership to onlookers. But, in reality, these moments of contention were their strength.

Think about it. Iron sharpens iron. These two fierce and brilliant women weren't clashing for ego or dominance. They clashed because they were passionate about the cause. Through this passionate discourse, their strategies evolved, became more refined, and, dare we say, more potent.

Each disagreement was a lesson. Stanton learned the value of patience and the art of timing from Anthony. Susan was repeatedly reminded of the larger picture, ensuring she stayed aware of the minutiae.

The bond between them was a testament to something profound: resolve. It was their shared resolve that navigated them through disagreements. Their eyes remained fixed on the prize, ensuring personal differences never overshadowed the larger cause.

And isn't that a lesson for us all? In our lives, disagreements are inevitable, whether in personal relationships, work, or activism. But the magic is the ability to see beyond the moment, recognize the shared goal, and use differences as stepping stones rather than stumbling blocks. That's the legacy Susan B. Anthony and Elizabeth Cady Stanton have gifted us. It's a call to embrace disagreements not as signs of discord but as opportunities for growth. How will you respond?

Chapter 4

The Revolution in Print

Imagine a world without instant communication. A place where a single printed word could spark revolutions, inspire movements or change the course of history. Now, transport yourself back to the 19th century, where the written word held immense power, and one woman stood at the forefront of this literary battle for equality: Susan B. Anthony.

Susan is the indomitable force behind the women's suffrage movement, but how many of us know her journey as a pioneering publisher? Amidst the clamor for women's rights, Susan understood something profound: lasting change would require impassioned speeches, public rallies, and the printed word.

Enter *The Revolution*. Does it sound like a daring name for a newspaper? Well, it was. Founded in 1868 by Susan and her close collaborator, Elizabeth Cady Stanton, this weekly periodical became the mouthpiece for women's rights. The newspaper's slogan? "Men, their rights, and nothing more; women, their rights, and nothing less." This wasn't just a catchphrase; it was a clarion call.

What was so special about *The Revolution*? For starters, it tackled taboo issues for its time: women's suffrage, marriage rights, divorce laws, and even birth control. Susan and Stanton understood the ripple effect of their words. In an era where women's voices were routinely silenced, each page of *The Revolution* shouted back, defying the norms.

But why take on the arduous task of publishing in an already crowded space? It's simple. Susan recognized the potency of the press. While speeches could rally those in attendance, printed words could reach thousands, if not millions, echoing across state lines and even oceans. The newspaper wasn't just about informing; it was about educating, persuading, and mobilizing.

However, like any monumental endeavor, *The Revolution* faced its fair share of challenges. Financial strains were perennial, with Susan digging into her pockets to keep the publication afloat. Criticism came thick and fast from detractors of the women's rights movement and fellow activists who deemed the paper too radical.

Yet, in every line of text, there was resilience. Every edition was a testament to Susan's unyielding spirit. Even when *The Revolution* ceased publication in 1872, its impact was undeniable. The conversations it started, the minds it changed, and the society it shaped: the echoes of *The Revolution* still resound today.

So, when we talk about Susan B. Anthony, let's not just remember her as a trailblazing activist but also as a media maverick. In the pages of *The Revolution*, we find a woman who realized early on that while voices could be hushed, the written word remained, waiting to inspire the next generation. What's more revolutionary than that?

Launching 'The Revolution'

In the turbulent heart of the 19th century, as societal waves crashed with demands for change and voices echoed with cries for equality, one woman stood steadfast, leading a charge that would shape the destiny of American women. Enter Susan B. Anthony, not just as an activist but as a media visionary.

Now, have you ever wondered what it takes to launch a revolution? Not just in spirit or in rallies but in print. It's not just about ink and paper; it's about carving out a platform, staking a claim, and crafting a message potent enough to stir souls. And in 1868, Susan did just that. But how?

In a world where the male-dominated media scarcely allowed a whisper of women's suffrage, Susan and her fierce collaborator Elizabeth Cady Stanton conceived *The Revolution*. No, not an uprising on the streets – though the essence wasn't far off – but a newspaper. A printed beacon for women's rights, rallying cries captured on paper, delivered weekly to the doorsteps of America.

Was the decision to helm a publication a strategic move or a leap of faith? A blend of both. The audacity of naming their periodical *The Revolution* spoke volumes. It signified defiance, determination, and a call to upturn deep-rooted conventions. And as you leaf through its pages, you're met with the paper's motto, bold and uncompromising: "Men, their rights, and nothing more; women, their rights, and nothing less."

For many, newspapers of the day offered news, perhaps entertainment. But for Susan and Stanton, *The Revolution* wasn't just a paper; it was a pulpit. From this platform, they tackled not just the vote but issues like marriage rights, education, and even the controversial topic of birth control. In a time when discussing such matters was taboo, Susan's audacity shone through. Can you feel the weight of that courage?

But as the pages of *The Revolution* turned week after week, it wasn't all accolades and smooth sailing. Financial challenges loomed large. Susan herself often bore the publication's financial burdens, revealing her unwavering commitment to the cause. And then there was criticism, not just from detractors, but from allies who felt their methods too aggressive, their tone too confrontational.

Yet, Susan pressed on. In every word printed, every edition published, *The Revolution* became more than just ink on paper. It became the voice of countless women, echoing their demands, aspirations, and dreams. It served as a testament that the written word can indeed launch revolutions when wielded with conviction.

Though *The Revolution* eventually folded in 1872, its legacy remains undiminished. Susan B. Anthony, with a paper and a dream, had cast a stone across the waters of a nation, creating ripples that would reshape its very fabric. And while today's battles for equality might differ, the spirit of *The Revolution* continues to inspire. For in its pages, one doesn't just read about history; one feels the heartbeat of a movement... And that, dear reader, is the magic of Susan B. Anthony's printed revolution!

Notable Columns and Controversies

Step back into the vibrant fabric of the 19th century, and there, against its backdrop, Susan B. Anthony emerges. This indomitable spirit wasn't just about speeches and public appearances; she also carved a niche in print. Ah, print! Do you ever pause to consider how the written word could ignite wildfires of thought before the age of viral tweets and trending hashtags?

"The Revolution," that audacious publication she co-founded with Elizabeth Cady Stanton, wasn't just an ordinary newspaper. It was a beacon, a pulsating heart broadcasting the rhythm of women's rights. And within its pages, some columns stood out, while others... well, they stirred the pot, rattling society's conventions.

Take, for example, the assertive declarations on the paper's masthead: "Men, their rights, and nothing more; women, their rights, and nothing less." Provocative? Absolutely. But Susan wasn't in the business of tiptoeing around sensitivities. Her message was clear and unwavering.

But what about the columns themselves? The article on women's " right to own property" resonated deeply. In a time when women were largely considered property, such a notion was revolutionary. And yet, there it was in print, questioning: Why shouldn't a woman control her earnings and land?

Another memorable piece was on the issue of marriage and divorce. Here, Susan and her team didn't just argue for legal rights but delved into the emotional and moral fabric of the society. They asked, should a woman be chained to a marriage, devoid of love or respect, simply because society dictates it?

However, the columns had their share of controversies. For instance, the publication's stance on birth control was met with a spectrum of reactions. Some readers championed the brave exploration of such a topic, while others, including staunch allies, raised eyebrows in the reservation. And then, there was the storm surrounding the paper's support for a controversial figure like Victoria Woodhull, who championed "free love." Some readers gasped, some cheered, but no one could ignore it.

In the realm of racial equality, the publication's waters grew murkier. Susan's commitment to women's rights was undeniable. Still, her willingness to sideline the fight for Black voting rights, especially after the Civil War, drew criticism. The publication's decision to prioritize women's suffrage over the Fifteenth Amendment, which granted Black men the right to vote, became a point of contention. Lines were drawn, allies became critics, and the discourse intensified.

Yet through every column every controversy, *The Revolution* maintained its essence: to challenge, provoke, and demand change. And Susan, with her unwavering spirit, ensured that every word, every sentence served its purpose: to jolt the reader from complacency, to make them question, to make them think...

Was Susan B. Anthony perfect? No. Did she shy away from controversy? Clearly not. But in the grand tapestry of history, amidst its shades of gray, her legacy, carved in ink and passion, remains an emblem of audacity and change!

Financial Strains and the Paper's Demise

In the echoing halls of history, where the drumbeat of change reverberates, we often find tales of soaring ideals and the very earthly struggles that define the human condition. Enter the story of *The Revolution*, the newspaper Susan B. Anthony birthed into existence alongside Elizabeth Cady Stanton. It wasn't merely a newspaper but a dream, a manifesto, a call to arms. But even the noblest of endeavors sometimes grapple with an old adversary: finances.

Money. It's the lifeline of any venture. And *The Revolution*, for all its ideological might, was no exception. From the outset, the paper's financial footing was precarious. Passion and purpose drove its engine, but capital? That remained an ever-elusive fuel.

If the content was so gripping, if the mission so crucial, why did the coffers run dry? The subscription model, though noble in intention, proved to be an Achilles' heel. Susan believed in keeping the paper free from the influence of advertisers, which, while ethically commendable, created financial limitations. The lack of advertising revenue meant that every copy printed, every article penned, rested heavily on subscriber support.

Anthony's commitment to the cause even saw her pour her personal funds into the venture. But how often can one dip into personal savings before the well dries? Even her lecture tours, captivating as they were, sometimes served more as fundraisers for the paper than platforms for the larger cause. One might wonder: Did she ever feel that burden of keeping a dream afloat amidst a sea of red?

Despite the passion, there were other elements at play. The paper's audacious content, while its biggest strength, became a double-edged sword. It garnered attention, but it also invited controversies, affecting its appeal to the broader masses. And though *The Revolution* echoed the sentiments of many, it also alienated potential allies, those who felt the paper's stance on certain issues was too radical.

Then came that fateful year, 1870. The realities of finance overpowered the dreams of reformers. *The Revolution*, after three tumultuous years, ceased its print run. Its voice, so bold, so defiant, fell silent. But was it truly the end?

In the annals of history, *The Revolution* might have met its material demise, but its spirit? That's another story. Its echoes continued to inspire countless souls, and undeterred Susan marched forward. After all, while papers might fold and money might wane, ideals, once ignited, burn forever.

Chapter 5

A Vote Cast, A Nation Stunned

How many times do we, in the quiet of our lives, dream of moments that will stir the very foundations of a nation? Often, these moments are unexpected, even for the ones who catalyze them. Susan B. Anthony was no stranger to causing ripples. Still, in 1872, she cast a stone that would send waves crashing through the American landscape.

Picture this: The United States is still mending its wounds from a civil war and is on the brink of an evolution. Women, though, are spectators in this land of the free. It's an age where the echo of the ballot dropping into the box is a sound only men know. But what happens when a woman, filled with conviction and armed with audacity, decides to cast her vote?

It was a chilly November morning in Rochester, New York. Susan B. Anthony, with a glint in her eyes and resolve in her stride, walked into a barbershop turned polling station. Can you sense the electricity in the air? It wasn't just another day; history was knocking.

She stood there, looking every bit the reformer she was. As she registered her vote, the room might have been silent, but for the scratching of the pen and the drop of the ballot, it felt like a thunderclap. The men present didn't know whether to be amazed, angered, or stupefied.

Let's not mistake this for a mere act of rebellion. This was a statement: a proclamation that women, too, had a voice, and it would be heard. It was a daring step, a vivid declaration, and the nation took notice!

But there were consequences. Anthony was arrested, facing a $100 fine she refused to pay. The trial that followed? It wasn't just about an illegal vote. It became a national conversation on women's rights. A spotlight had been shone, and under its glare, the cracks in the system became painfully evident.

While the vote itself was but a blip in that year's election, it left an indelible mark on the psyche of a nation. Questions arose. Debates raged. If a woman, educated and aware, is not allowed to vote, where does democracy stand? This audacious act, this singular vote, laid the groundwork for the 19th Amendment. This law would eventually grant women the right to vote.

Susan's act of defiance, that moment in the barbershop, remains a testament to the power of individual action. It reminds us that grand gestures and massive rallies sometimes bring about change. Sometimes, it begins with one person deciding they won't be silent anymore.

So, the next time you're at a crossroads, wondering if your solitary voice matters, remember Susan B. Anthony. Remember that chilly November day. And ask yourself: If she could shake a nation with a single vote, what could you do with your voice? The possibilities are limitless.

1872: The Act of Defiance

In the tapestry of history, some threads glisten brighter than others, moments when an individual action echoes louder than countless speeches. 1872 held one such moment, a silent act of defiance by Susan B. Anthony. But why was this year significant, and how did a single act galvanize a movement?

Let's step back in time. The United States, still reeling from the effects of the Civil War, was undergoing significant change. Reconstruction was underway, but not all citizens participated in this "rebirth." Women, constituting half of the population, were muted spectators, their voices stifled, their rights ignored.

Susan B. Anthony was different from the kind of woman to idly stand by. Having campaigned for abolition and temperance, she was no stranger to a challenge. But what can one woman do in the face of an entire system?

As Americans prepared to cast their ballots, November came with its crisp autumn air. Susan was among the men making their way to the polling booths in Rochester, New York. Can you feel the tension as she steps up? With her heart probably racing and a stern look on her face, Susan did the unthinkable. She voted.

It might seem like a small act today, but imagine the scene! The hushed murmurs, the incredulous stares, the sheer audacity of a woman exercising her civic duty in a society that had explicitly barred her from it.

What followed was inevitable. The law swung its hammer, and Susan B. Anthony was arrested. Yet, isn't it often in the crucible of adversity that true character shines? Instead of wilting, Susan transformed her trial into a national spectacle, a platform. The courtroom resonated with her voice as she articulated a question many had chosen to ignore: Why shouldn't a woman vote? Why, in a land priding itself on democracy, was half its populace denied a basic right?

The trial culminated with Susan being fined $100, a sum she refused to pay. But it wasn't about the money; it was about the message. And the message was loud and clear: change was imminent.

For Susan, 1872 wasn't just about casting a vote; it was about casting a vision for the future. A vision where women would stand shoulder to shoulder with men, not as subordinates but as equals.

The aftermath of that act was profound. People debated, criticized, and pondered across parlors, in newspapers, and on the streets. And while the 19th Amendment, granting women the right to vote, would only materialize decades later, the spark had been ignited.

When discussing acts of defiance, it's easy to conjure images of grand gestures, massive rallies, and loud protests. But sometimes, defiance is quiet, subtle, and deeply personal. It's a woman walking up to a ballot box, insisting on her place in history. Susan B. Anthony, in 1872, didn't just vote for a candidate; she voted for change. And in doing so, she taught us all a valuable lesson: never underestimate the power of a single act fueled by conviction. Who knows what ripples it might create?

Trials and Tribulations

There's a pulse to history, a rhythm that beats through time. And within this cadence are moments of pause, of deep breaths taken before plunging into the tumultuous waters of change. Such was the ambiance when Susan B. Anthony, a name now synonymous with women's rights, stepped into a courtroom in 1873.

Can you imagine it? The courtroom buzzing with anticipation, the air thick with tension. Here stood a defiant yet dignified woman in a space where few women dared to tread. This wasn't just any trial; it was a spectacle, a performance, a dance between tradition and progress.

Why was she here? Recall that Susan had committed a simple yet groundbreaking act a year prior: she'd voted. A woman casting a ballot might sound almost pedestrian to our ears today. But back then? It was revolutionary. And, like most revolutions, it was met with resistance.

As the charges against her were read out, Susan must have felt the weight of more than just her actions. On her shoulders rested the dreams of countless women yearning for a voice, a say in the very fabric of their nation. But facing accusations and a possible fine, did doubt ever creep in? Did she second-guess her actions, wondering if she'd gone too far?

Yet, as the proceedings unfolded, it became abundantly clear: Susan B. Anthony was no ordinary defendant. She didn't cower; she soared. With eloquence and enthusiasm, Susan defended not only her act of voting but also the broader principle of women's suffrage. Every word she spoke, and argument she put forth weren't just for her benefit and for women everywhere.

"How can the 'consent of the governed' be given," she questioned, "if that right is denied to half the population?" It is a simple question but one that rattled the cages of tradition.

The courtroom drama culminated in a $100 fine for Susan. But money wasn't the real issue here. Principle was. And in true Anthony fashion, she declared she'd never pay a penny of that unjust fine. Why should she when the very foundation of the case against her was flawed?

While the gavel declared her guilty, history would vindicate her. With its high ceilings and wooden pews, that courtroom wasn't just a place of judgment; it was a stage. And Susan? She wasn't merely a defendant but a protagonist in a larger narrative, pushing boundaries and challenging the status quo.

Ultimately, Susan B. Anthony's trial was more than a legal proceeding. It was a message, a clarion call to women everywhere: Stand up, speak out, and let not the challenges deter you. In facing the court, Susan didn't just defend herself; she championed a cause, igniting a fire that would eventually light up the entire nation. And what could be more human, more genuine, than a woman standing up against the tides, challenging the waves that sought to push her back?

A Nation Divided

Imagine a nation on the cusp of change, a landscape where the very foundations of democracy trembled. Here, Susan B. Anthony planted her flag, marking her claim in the struggle for women's rights. But how did the public react? How did a nation respond when one woman dared to challenge the status quo?

As news of Anthony's bold actions spread, the United States found itself pulled in two directions. On one side, applause and admiration echoed from every corner. Newspapers championed her spirit, women across the country drew inspiration, and countless supporters rallied behind her. They saw in Susan not just a rebel but a beacon, illuminating the path toward equality.

Yet, not all applause is met without its share of boos. Resistance, as they say, is a testament to progress. And Susan's quest was no different.

Some quarters painted her as a radical, a threat to the very fabric of society. Families gathered around dinner tables, where debates raged, and voices clashed. Men in smoky taverns questioned: what would become of the country if women began to vote? And what would that mean for their own roles?

It was during this period that a particular incident stood out. After casting her fateful vote, Susan was confronted by an angry man outside the polling booth. He exclaimed, "A woman's place is in the home, not the voting line!" But Susan, ever the beacon of calm and reason, responded, "And who, sir, determines that place if not us?"

The nation's newspapers became battlegrounds. Columns, articles, and caricatures filled the pages, each staking their claim in the ongoing debate. Was Susan B. Anthony a hero or a heretic? Was she the future or a dangerous diversion?

Interestingly, this division wasn't merely along gender lines. Many women, perhaps conditioned by the times or protective of their perceived roles, viewed Susan's actions with suspicion. On the other hand, a sizable number of men stood with her, advocating for a shared vision of equality.

Amidst this cacophony of opinions, one thing was evident: Susan B. Anthony had ignited a spark that would set the nation ablaze. This wasn't just about a woman's right to vote; it was about the identity of a country, about the principles it upheld, and the future it envisioned.

By demanding her rights, Susan did more than assert her societal place. She forced the nation to confront its own contradictions. The question wasn't just whether women should vote. It was deeper, more introspective: what kind of nation did America want to be?

In this tapestry of reactions, it's essential to remember that public sentiment is never monolithic. It ebbs and flows, shaped by personal experiences, societal norms, and the winds of change. And while Susan B. Anthony may not have won every heart or changed every mind, she certainly set the wheels in motion, ensuring that the conversation, once started, would never truly end.

Chapter 6

Global Reverberations

Imagine the world, vast and interconnected, yet fragmented by beliefs, cultures, and traditions. How does one voice, echoing from the shores of one nation, traverse these divides to inspire hearts globally? Such was the power of Susan B. Anthony's indomitable spirit.

The tremors of her fight against inequality weren't confined merely within the borders of America. Far beyond, in towns and cities across continents, whispers began to spread. Who was this woman who stood resolute against the tidal wave of conventions? And how did her actions reverberate across the world?

From the bustling streets of London to the quiet corners of rural India, Susan B. Anthony's name became synonymous with resistance, hope, and change. She inspired women from different cultures, backgrounds, and beliefs to question their prescribed roles and to ponder, why not them? Why couldn't they demand equality in voting, employment, and life?

Consider, for a moment, the tea rooms of England. Women gathered, sipping their afternoon brews, their conversations drifting from daily chores to this American rebel. "Have you heard of Susan B. Anthony?" one might ask, her eyes alight with newfound enthusiasm. Another might respond, "Yes, and if she can, why can't?"

Similarly, across the vast plains of Africa, stories of SSusan'sbattles began to weave into the fabric of local legends. Mothers and grandmothers would recount tales of this distant woman, using her narrative to instill a sense of purpose and empowerment in their young daughters.

Further east, the ripples of her impact touched even the most isolated regions. In villages where traditions ran deep and change was often viewed with suspicion, a quiet transformation began to take root. Leaders and thinkers in these communities began to use Anthony's narrative as a backdrop for dialogue on women's women rights. "America can begin to rethink its stance. Why can't?""

Susan's story became a global testament to the idea that change is possible, even in the face of impossible odds. Her journey offered hope, illuminating a path for women worldwide who dared to dream of a more egalitarian society.

It is crucial to understand that while Susan B. Anthony became a symbol of hope, her influence was a double-edged sword. While many found inspiration, others saw her ideals threatening their societal structure. But isn't that the true hallmark of a revolutionary? Someone who champions change and forces others to confront and question their long-held beliefs?

In the annals of history, many names fade with time, their legacies lost in the sand of ages. But Susan B. Anthony's impact felt from the heartlands of the U.S. to the far reaches of the globe ensures that her legacy remains timeless. She didn't just change a nation; she inspired the world. And that, dear reader, is the true essence of global reverberation.

The International Council of Women

Imagine an era when oceans were more than just expanses of water; they were barriers to ideas, movements, and connections. Now, picture a woman determined enough to cross that ocean, both literally and metaphorically. Susan B. Anthony wasn't just content with sparking a revolution at home; her aspirations transcended national boundaries.

The year was 1888. While most would be contemplating a quiet life, Anthony was brewing another storm. This time on international waters. What might drive someone to push boundaries at this age? Simple: the belief that equality knows no borders.

As co-founder of The International Council of Women (ICW), Anthony sought to unite the world's suffragists under one banner. But why is this significant, you ask?

Consider the global landscape of the late 19th century. Countries were silos, with women's rights movements operating in isolation. Information didn't stream instantly into our pockets; it traveled at the speed of ships. In such times, envision the audacity of Anthony's dream: a global consortium of women standing united.

The ICW was not just another conference; it was a statement. Women from different cultures, religions, and races assembled in Washington, D.C., answering Anthony's clarion call. They shared, learned, and strategized. Their unity, in itself, was a powerful message to the world. If women from diverse backgrounds could find common ground, why couldn't they?

The conversations at the ICW were groundbreaking. From women's suffrage to educational rights, property rights, and employment opportunities, the discourse was rich, varied, and ahead of its time. But beyond the specific issues, a broader narrative was taking shape—a narrative of global sisterhood.

How did societies react to this? In parts of Europe, leaders dismissed it as a fanciful American experiment. Yet, behind closed doors, they were introspective. Could their nations afford to ignore this rising tide of female empowerment? And if they did, at what cost?

For many attendees, the ICW wasn't just an event but an awakening. They returned to their home countries, not just as delegates but as ambassadors of a global movement. Inspired by Anthony's vision, they began establishing local chapters, sewing the seeds of change. Women from New Zealand to Argentina felt a kinship: they were all part of Anthony's grand tapestry.

The genius of Susan B. Anthony lay not just in her ability to rally women but in her foresight. She understood that for women's rights to take root truly, they had to be universal. By founding the ICW, she was bridging the Atlantic and building bridges between women worldwide.

Today, when we think of globalization, we think of technology, trade, and travel. But isn't it fascinating to realize that over a century ago, globalization had another face? A face determined, unwavering, and brimming with conviction: that of Susan B. Anthony.

Ultimately, Anthony's legacy isn't just about the rights she championed and the global community she envisaged—a community where every woman, no matter her origin, believed in a shared dream. And if you ever wonder about the power of one individual's vision, think of Anthony. From the streets of Rochester to the corridors of the ICW, her echo is timeless. How is that for crossing oceans?

Global Suffrage Movements

If you will, picture the world of the late 19th and early 20th century. It was a time when voices emerged from the shadows, demanding change, seeking justice, and roaring for equality. In the heart of this tumultuous period, one woman's name resounded louder than most: Susan B. Anthony.

How did one American woman's ambition reverberate beyond her homeland's homeland's homeland's homeland's homeland's homeland's borders? The answer lies not just in her convictions but in her keen sense to learn and share. For Anthony, the suffrage movement was never confined to the streets of America. She envisioned a world where every woman, regardless of nationality, race, or creed, had a voice.

Anthony's initial endeavors began at home, yes. But as she deepened her understanding of the suffrage movement, she realized a profound truth: injustice anywhere threatened justice everywhere. Isn't it fascinating that while oceans divided nations, the thirst for equality united women across continents?

She often corresponded with global suffrage leaders like Emily Davison of Britain and Henrietta Dugdale of Australia. Through letters, they shared strategies, setbacks, and stories. Can you imagine their excitement with each envelope they received? These were just letters, lifelines of hope, encouragement, and camaraderie.

While America had challenges, other nations painted a different backdrop for their suffrage stories. In New Zealand, women claimed the right to vote in 1893, becoming the first self-governing country to grant national suffrage to women. Across the globe, in Finland, women won the right to vote in 1906 and stood as candidates in elections.

And Anthony? She absorbed these tales of triumph and turbulence. She celebrated every victory and mourned each setback in Europe, Asia, or down under. But beyond just absorbing, she propagated. She championed the successes of the global suffrage movement, using them as catalysts to fuel America's drive.

A crucial moment arrived when Anthony co-founded The International Council of Women in 1888. Do you realize the audacity of this endeavor? The council didn't just aim to address suffrage. It dreamt bigger. From educational rights to employment equality, it tackled issues we are still grappling with over a century later. For Anthony, voting was the start, not the end.

The beauty of Susan B. Anthony's involvement with global suffrage movements lay in her ability to be both student and teacher. She imbibed lessons from her global counterparts, incorporated them into the American struggle, and simultaneously showcased the American journey to inspire women worldwide.

It's easy to see Anthony as an American icon, and she is. But confining her to just that diminishes the scope of her vision and legacy. In truth, she was a global citizen. One might even dare to say: a pioneer of globalization, not in trade or technology, but in ideals, dreams, and the ceaseless pursuit of equality.

So, the next time you think of Susan B. Anthony, remember: her fight wasn't bound by geography. She looked beyond the horizon, understanding that shared struggles and mutual learning paved the path to a better world. And in doing so, she left footprints not just on American soil but on the sands of time worldwide. Is that a legacy worth celebrating?

Incorporating International Strategies

Step back into the 19th century and consider: What did it mean for a woman in the United States, or anywhere in the world, to raise her voice for her rights? Susan B. Anthony knew and wasn't just focused on her backyard. Think about it: When fighting for a cause bigger than yourself, isn't it wise to gather perspectives beyond your horizon?

Susan's home was in America, yes, but her eyes? They were fixed firmly on the globe. How could one champion the cause of women's suffrage and not consider the plight and progress of women across oceans and continents?

Britain was buzzing with the suffrage movement. The suffragettes there made headlines with their daring protests and hunger strikes. And Anthony? She took note. Their motto, "deeds, not words," resonated deeply with her. How could it not? Every time a British suffragette was imprisoned, Anthony felt that same cage rattle in America. When Emmeline Pankhurst rallied her countrywomen, Anthony took to heart the message of direct action and civil disobedience. It wasn't about copying strategies but drawing inspiration and adapting them to the American context.

But it wasn't just Britain. Anthony looked to the distant shores of New Zealand, where women were casting their votes as early as 1893. And to Finland, where, come 1906, women not only voted but stood as electoral candidates! Can you grasp the audacity of such moves in that era? Anthony did. Each success story abroad infused the American movement with renewed vigor and possibility.

Her correspondence was her gateway to the world. Through letters – those beautifully crafted, hand-written messages – Anthony bridged the Atlantic and beyond. Each envelope she opened brought tales of strategies tried, challenges faced, and victories celebrated. And each letter she penned back carried the essence of the American fight, echoing hope and determination.

Now, consider France. Its cafes were not just places of leisure but hubs of political discourse. In those very cafes, Susan B. Anthony met with French activists. Over cups of coffee, strategies were debated, experiences were exchanged, and an international camaraderie was forged. If an idea worked in

France, why not introduce it in America, albeit with a local flavor? And if something faltered in the U.S., the lesson was there for her French counterparts to learn from.

One must wonder: Did Anthony ever feel overwhelmed by this global outlook? But here's the thing: She understood that voting wasn't a solitary struggle. The waves of a stone thrown in Europe could create ripples in America.

So, as the sun set each evening in Susan B. Anthony's homeland, it rose over another part of the world where women were rallying for their rights. And Anthony, with her global perspective, ensured that every ray of hope, every strategy devised, and every victory achieved abroad illuminated the path for women at home.

In today's instant communication, such global collaboration might seem obvious. But back then? It was revolutionary. And in the heart of that revolution stood Susan B. Anthony, always looking outward, always learning, and always ensuring that the fight for women's suffrage was, at its core, a shared global endeavor. How about broadening one's horizons?

Chapter 7

Facing the Fire: Overcoming Opposition

Imagine walking a path strewn with thorns, and with every step you take, the pricks become more pointed, the cuts deeper. This, in essence, was the journey of Susan B. Anthony. With the flames of opposition burning brightly against her, Anthony didn't just tread that dangerous path; she did so with conviction, grace, and unwavering courage.

Now, it's tempting to paint a rosy picture where our heroine easily triumphs against all odds. But reality, as we well know, has its rough edges. Anthony's struggles were real, tangible. From society's whispers of disdain to shouts of outright hatred, opposition met her at every corner. And yet, isn't it true that the fiercest fires forge the strongest steel?

When the men at the ballot boxes laughed in her face, the newspapers mocked her efforts, and even fellow suffragists questioned her methods, Anthony faced the fire head-on. And do you know what kept her going? A belief, rock-solid and deep-rooted: the belief that every woman had a rightful place in the fabric of democracy.

With Elizabeth Cady Stanton by her side, Anthony crafted strategies. But it wasn't always about grand gestures and sweeping statements. Sometimes, resistance was in the quiet acts: a conversation over tea, a letter penned late at night, or a speech delivered to a room half-empty but with hearts fully engaged. These seemingly small acts laid the groundwork for a change that was monumental.

However, facing resistance wasn't just about navigating external obstacles. The internal battles, the moments of doubt: those, too, were part and parcel of Anthony's journey. Have you ever thought of how many nights she might've lain awake, pondering if the path she chose was too rugged or unforgiving? But morning always brought clarity: the cause was just, the fight was necessary, and surrender? It was never an option.

As opposition grew, so did Anthony's resolve. Arrested for voting in 1872, she could've cowered and felt defeated. But did she? Instead, that courtroom became a stage, her trial a platform. With eloquence and fervor, Anthony defended not just herself but every woman's right to vote. And the ripple effects of that act? They're still felt today.

So, what can we learn from Susan B. Anthony's dance with opposition? It may be this: One can retreat or rise when faced with adversity. Anthony chose the latter. She faced the flames, stood tall amidst the roaring fires of opposition, and emerged not burnt but shining brighter than ever.

Isn't that the kind of legacy we all hope to leave behind? And as we navigate our own challenges, might we, too, find the strength to face our fires, just as Anthony did, with grace, grit, and an unyielding spirit. After all, isn't that the essence of true resilience?

The Press and Public Perception

In an era where the clatter of typewriters echoed like the rhythm of progress, Susan B. Anthony was both a beacon and a target. The press, that formidable entity of her time, didn't simply report on her actions; they shaped the very narrative of her journey. How did a world of ink and paper influence the life of one of the most audacious women in history?

Step into the late 19th century. The air buzzes with conversations, debates, and a hint of revolution? Newspapers, the lifeblood of information, flowed freely. Susan B. Anthony's actions frequently adorned their pages. Sometimes, she was the heroine: a woman daring to challenge conventions. Other times, the villain is a disruptor seeking to upend the societal order.

Perhaps more than anyone of her time, Anthony understood the weight that public perception carried. A single headline could shape the opinions of thousands. And so, she cultivated relationships with reporters. Was it manipulation? No. It was strategy. It was an understanding that one had to first win minds to win hearts. And where do minds often turn for guidance? The headlines, the op-eds, the evening paper.

Every speech she gave, every rally she led, Anthony knew the press watched, their pens poised. But instead of shying away, she leaned in. She engaged them with her eloquence and won them over with her convictions. Even when the press vilified her, Anthony saw an opportunity. Controversy, after all, sparks interest. And interest paves the way for dialogue.

And what of the public? They are, after all, the sea in which the press casts its net. Public perception shifted as Anthony's name became synonymous with the suffrage movement. Anthony's influence was palpable, from the woman who sat at her breakfast table reading about Anthony's latest endeavors to the young girl who hung on every word of her speeches. The press played its role: amplifying, critiquing, debating. And the public, ever the keen observer, began to form their own judgments.

Yet, it wasn't always rosy. Anthony had her fair share of detractors. Every article praising her efforts was often met with another tearing them down. But isn't that the nature of change? Resistance meets persistence. And Susan B. Anthony was nothing if not persistent.

It's curious to think: What would Anthony have made of today's digital age, where opinions form and dissipate with a button? One can only speculate. But in her time, in her world of ink and paper, she navigated the delicate dance between the press and public perception with a finesse that was nothing short of masterful.

As readers, thinkers, and members of society, we, too, have a role. In an age of information overload, might we take a page out of Anthony's book? To look beyond the headlines, form our own perceptions, and engage in the discourse of our times. After all, isn't that the very essence of an informed democracy?

Rifts Within

Have you ever walked into a room filled with passion and enthusiasm? If you could, imagine the late 19th century, a time of corsets and top hats, where the battle for women's rights raged with fiery intensity beneath the decorum. It wasn't just a battle against the established norms; sometimes, the fiercest battles were fought within the ranks. Enter the world of Susan B. Anthony and the tussle between two colossal institutions: The National Women's Suffrage Association (NWSA) and the American Women's Suffrage Association (AWSA).

The air was thick with aspiration. Women nationwide rallied for the right to vote, and two major associations emerged. But why two? Why not a united front? The very crux of the matter lies in strategy and philosophy.

The NWSA, co-founded by Susan B. Anthony and Elizabeth Cady Stanton, often took the road less traveled. Their approach was radical, even for some suffragettes. They believed in a federal amendment, a sweeping change that would grant women nationwide the right to vote. But their ambitions didn't stop there. Beyond voting, they aimed to challenge and reshape other societal norms, addressing issues like marital rights and divorce laws.

Contrast that with the AWSA. More conservative, this association, led by Lucy Stone and Julia Ward Howe, believed in a state-by-state approach. Win the states, and the nation will follow, they argued. Their focus was laser-sharp: voting rights and nothing more. For them, broader societal changes were for another day, another fight.

But let's step back. Why should this rift matter to us? Because, dear reader, it reminds us of the age-old truth: even within a revolution, there are revolutions. People's beliefs and dreams rarely align perfectly; sometimes, they clash spectacularly. Susan B. Anthony, ever the strategist, often found herself in the eye of this storm.

Imagine the conversations, the debates. With her firebrand style, Anthony advocates for the broader, all-encompassing change. Conversely, the AWSA members, with their pragmatic approach, urged for focus. The tension wasn't just ideological; it was deeply personal. Friends became rivals. Allies, adversaries.

Yet, amidst this fierce rivalry, a realization dawned. To win the war, battles of ego and ideology had to be set aside. And so, in 1890, these two associations merged with all their differences to form the National American Women's Suffrage Association (NAWSA). Anthony, ever the leader, became its first president.

Such is the nature of movements. They ebb and flow. They rupture and mend. But the heart of the story? It's not about the rifts but the bridges built over them. It reminds us that even in discord, there's an opportunity for unity and harmony.

So, as we reflect on the journey of Susan B. Anthony and the tumultuous path of women's suffrage, we're left with a question: In our pursuits, do we let differences deter us, or do we, like Anthony, find a way to weave them into a tapestry of progress? The choice, as always, remains ours.

Reconciliation and Progress

In the tapestry of Susan B. Anthony's life, where threads of activism, courage, and tenacity intertwine, a hue often gets overshadowed. A shade that symbolizes unity. A color of reconciliation. Unfortunately, divisions had painted a picture of discord in the realm of voting. But was this divide insurmountable? Or did Susan find a way to stitch the differences together?

To understand the gravity of this unification, one must first step back into the midst of the conflict. Two associations: The National Women's Suffrage Association (NWSA) and the American Women's Suffrage Association (AWSA). Their motives were the same, yet their paths were worlds apart. While the former, led by Anthony and Stanton, championed a bold, national approach, the latter preferred the steadiness of a state-by-state stride. And as with any genuine cause, emotions ran high, causing ripples of disagreement.

But here's where our story takes an intriguing twist. Amidst this tumult, Anthony, the ever-persistent visionary, realized something profound: the weight of unity in the face of adversity. How could one swim against the societal tide with weights of disagreement shackling the feet?

The 1890s bore witness to this revelation. A merger. A coming together of two giants. The National American Women's Suffrage Association (NAWSA) was born, and the spirit of compromise and collaboration lay in its very formation. At its helm? Susan B. Anthony. It's no coincidence that the woman, who had been at the forefront of the divide, now stood as the beacon of unity.

Why did she do it? Was it merely for the sake of political expediency? Or was there something more... human at play? Think of the personal relationships, the friendships that had weathered the storm of disagreement. Think of the shared dreams, the collective aspirations momentarily clouded by the fog of dispute. By uniting these associations, Anthony wasn't just forging an organizational alliance; she was mending broken bonds and bridging emotional rifts. It was a testament to her belief in the power of togetherness.

And the results spoke for themselves. NAWSA, under the guidance of Susan and other formidable leaders, became a force to reckon with. Their campaigns gained momentum, their voice echoing louder in the halls of power. Once seen as radical, the dream of a constitutional amendment was inching closer to reality. A unified voice, after all, is more to pay attention to.

So, as we traverse the annals of history, walking alongside figures like Susan B. Anthony, we're often left with nuggets of wisdom. One such lesson, stark in its simplicity, is this: in unity, there's strength. And while disagreements are but a natural course of any endeavor, it's the ability to rise above, to come together for a shared cause, that truly marks progress.

Isn't that what we all strive for? Don't we seek that harmony in our lives and societies? Susan B. Anthony's journey reminds us there's always room for reconciliation, even amidst the most passionate debates. At the end of the day, progress is not just about marching forward but ensuring no one is left behind. And who better than Susan to teach us that?

Chapter 8

A Voice that Echoed: Anthony's Words

In the landscape of America's awakening to women's rights, few voices carried the resonance of Susan B. Anthony. Picture a time when women were mostly silent spectators in the gallery of democracy, their aspirations muffled by the curtains of tradition. Then imagine a voice, clear and uncompromising, piercing that silence. That voice belonged to Susan. But what was it about her words that left an indelible mark on the fabric of history?

Susan's words were not mere utterances. They were her soul, captured in phrases and sentences, painting a vivid picture of a world where justice wasn't a luxury but a right. Have you ever heard a speech that gave you chills? That made the hair on your arms stand? Anthony's addresses had such power. It wasn't just about what she said but how she said it.

Every word she chose was a careful selection, a missile aimed at the prejudices of her time. When she stated, "Men, their rights, and nothing more; women, their rights, and nothing less," the nation paused. Such brevity! Such clarity! It was as if she had distilled the essence of the movement into a singular, potent dose.

But the magnetism of Susan's rhetoric didn't just reside in its content. It was the emotion, the conviction behind each word. Listeners often remarked how, when she spoke, it was impossible not to be drawn in. They felt she wasn't just speaking to a crowd but to each individual, addressing their innermost fears and hopes. That's the magic of genuine communication. When words transcend the barriers of paper and sound and touch the listener's very soul.

Let's remember her letters, those treasures of personal insight. In an era without the immediacy of today's digital communication, letters were the lifelines of connection. And Susan's letters? They were revelations. Through them, we see the activist and the woman: her doubts, joys, and moments of introspection.

Her collaboration with Elizabeth Cady Stanton was a testament to the might of shared vision. Their exchanges, rich with ideas and strategies, provide a fascinating glimpse into the mechanics of a movement in the making. These letters weren't just dispatches but the building blocks of history.

But why does Anthony's voice still matter today? Why do her words still echo in discussions, debates, and discourses? It may be because true passion is timeless. When someone speaks from the heart, with authenticity and purpose, their words attain a kind of immortality.

Consider this: over a century has passed, and here we are, still talking about her, quoting her, still inspired by her. In a world constantly evolving, where yesterday's news is forgotten by today, the endurance of her voice is nothing short of miraculous. It's a testament to the power of words spoken with sincerity and conviction.

So, as we reflect on the legacy of Susan B. Anthony, let's remember that it wasn't just about her actions, vital as they were. It was also about her words, those pearls of wisdom and defiance. For in her voice, many found their own. In her words, many found their path. And isn't that the greatest gift of all: to inspire, empower, echo through time?

The Speeches That Moved the Masses

Step into any room where Susan B. Anthony stood tall, and you'd instantly feel a charge in the air. You know those rare individuals who command attention without even trying? Susan was one of them. She didn't just talk; she spoke to the heart, evoking a sense of urgency and inspiring action with every word that spilled from her lips.

Few names shine brighter when one speaks of oratory prowess in suffrage than Susan's. The stage was her domain, the audience, her canvas. But what was it about her speeches that left such an indelible mark?

Each time Susan ascended a platform, it wasn't just about presenting a viewpoint. It was about weaving a narrative, constructing a bridge of empathy. The words she chose the way she delivered them, all testified to a life spent in passionate advocacy. And for what? The audacious belief that women deserved equal rights.

In her groundbreaking speech, "Is it a Crime for a Citizen of the United States to Vote?" Susan tossed a simple question to her audience. But its simplicity bore the weight of centuries of gender inequality. She deftly brought attention to a core contradiction: How could a nation built on the ideals of freedom and democracy so blatantly disregard half of its population?

Remember her iconic address at the Women's Suffrage Convention in Washington? With utmost precision, she juxtaposed the Declaration of Independence with the prevalent gender norms. "All men and women are created equal," she started, emphasizing 'and women' with a force that left an echo. Her aim? To stir something primal within the hearts of her listeners.

But Susan's speeches were more than mere words. They were beacons of hope, serving as the North Star for countless women navigating the murky waters of gender bias. Her words were an invitation, urging them to join her in a dance of defiance against societal conventions. And boy, did they dance!

However, it wasn't all about grand stages and vast audiences. Some of Susan's most impactful words were spoken in intimate settings, in quiet town halls, or among small groups of women eager to bring about change. Though seemingly insignificant in the grand tapestry of her life, these moments were the sparks that ignited countless mini-revolutions.

What's fascinating is the relatability of her content. Susan's words transcended time and space. Even today, snippets of her speeches can be found emblazoned on placards, murals, and

T-shirts, a testament to their timeless relevance. Her voice resonates, encouraging modern-day warriors to pick up the baton and sprint forward.

But why did her speeches strike such a chord? Perhaps because they were birthed from authenticity. Every phrase, every pause, every inflection mirrored her own experiences, her own battles. Susan didn't speak from a pedestal; she spoke from the trenches, hand in hand with her fellow suffragettes.

Imagine being in her presence as she passionately articulated visions of a world where women walked shoulder to shoulder with men, their voices echoing in unison. The energy, the enthusiasm: it was palpable. With every sentence, she painted vivid strokes of a future ripe with possibilities.

So, take a moment next time you come across an excerpt from one of Susan's speeches. Dive deep into her words, let them wash over you. And as you emerge, you'll realize that Susan B. Anthony wasn't just a speaker. She was a force, a whirlwind of conviction, a beacon of change. And her speeches? They weren't mere words; they were revolutions wrapped in eloquence. Quite something.

Letters of Passion and Strategy

We often look at Susan B. Anthony through the lens of her public appearances, her tireless activism, and her speeches. But did you know another side to her reveals deeper layers? Dive into her personal letters, and you'll discover the heart and strategy that fueled her fight.

In our world of instant messaging and rapid email exchanges, it's easy to forget that letters were once the backbone of communication. For Susan, these weren't just modes of communication; they were lifelines. Imagine the care and attention required to dip a pen in ink and craft each word meticulously on paper. Each letter Anthony wrote carried weight, purpose, and emotion.

One could almost visualize Susan sitting at her wooden desk, the dim light of a lantern dancing on her pages as she enthusiastically penned her thoughts. These letters? They're a masterclass in both passion and strategy. Susan laid out her plans with every stroke of her pen, rallied her troops, and bared her soul.

For instance, her exchanges with her close ally, Elizabeth Cady Stanton. These weren't casual chit-chat. Theirs was a dialogue rich with ideas, enthusiasm, and tactical plotting. Within these letters, the blueprint for the women's suffrage movement was initially drafted. Can you sense the urgency in their exchanges? The unwavering resolve?

Yet, there's a more tender side to be found, too. Susan's letters to her family and friends often teemed with raw emotion: the joys, the setbacks, the moments of self-doubt, and the bursts of renewed vigor. These letters present a woman who felt deeply and bore the weight of her mission, not just in public arenas but in solitude and moments of reflection.

It's interesting to ponder: What fuels a revolution? Is it just the public rallies, the speeches that echo in grand halls? Or is it also these quieter moments, where strategies are birthed in handwritten words, where personal passions are laid bare on paper?

While we rightly celebrate her more visible contributions, let's recognize this treasure trove of letters. They chronicle the mind of a strategic genius and the heart of a woman driven by an unwavering sense of purpose. In every line and word, you can almost hear her heartbeat, feel the warmth of her breath, and sense the intensity of her gaze. Isn't it fascinating that words penned so long ago can still pulse with life, inspire, and draw us into Susan's world?

These letters, this personal correspondence, provide the most intimate bridge to Susan B. Anthony. They remind us that behind every movement, behind every call for change, there's a deeply personal story, a narrative crafted not just in public speeches but in the silent hours of introspection and strategy. And as we delve into these pages, we come face to face with Susan: the strategist, the dreamer, the woman... the legend.

Co-authoring the "History of Woman Suffrage"

When you think of monumental works that chart the course of history, few resonate as powerfully as the "History of Woman Suffrage." And behind this magnum opus? A union of minds, a confluence of energies. Here, we step into the collaborative journey of Susan B. Anthony and her notable peers in bringing this work to life.

Isn't it fascinating how some collaborations are almost destined? As if the universe conspires to bring together great minds to birth something transformative. Such was the case when Susan teamed up with Elizabeth Cady Stanton and Matilda Joslyn Gage. It wasn't just about pooling resources; it was about melding visions. How did these women, each powerful in her own right, come to write this pivotal document together?

The beginning is as simple as it is profound. These women saw a gaping hole in recorded history: the conspicuous absence of women's voices. Their struggles, achievements, and stories were mere footnotes or, worse, entirely absent. It begged the question: Who will tell our story? And the answer emerged: Why not us?

Each of these women brought something unique to the table. Stanton, with her incisive rhetoric; Gage, with her historical perspective; and Anthony? Her dogged determination and vast network of contacts ensured the creation and dissemination of this vital work. Anthony took on the mantle of ensuring the work reached the masses, tapping into her unparalleled organizing abilities to fund and promote the volumes.

It's critical to understand that this wasn't merely an academic exercise. The "History of Woman Suffrage" was strategic. It was a way to consolidate the suffrage movement's gains, document the journey, and provide a roadmap for the battles ahead. It was a manifesto and a history combined.

In those ink-stained pages, readers encountered personal letters, impassioned speeches, and detailed accounts of conventions and events. The collaborative effort spanned decades, resulting in multiple volumes that bore testament to the changing tides of the suffrage movement. The endeavor was monumental, and the process was fraught with challenges. Remember, these were the days before instant messaging and video calls. Coordination was through letters, face-to-face meetings, and a shared commitment to the cause. Can you imagine the hours spent, the letters exchanged, the drafts debated?

Yet, as with all great collaborations, it wasn't without tensions. Creative differences arose, as they often do when strong minds converge. But the disagreements were not the story; the unity of purpose was. Despite the challenges, the trio, along with the help of many other suffragists, produced a work that would serve as the primary resource on women's suffrage for generations to come.

Today, as we leaf through the "History of Woman Suffrage," we encounter more than just facts. We touch the very soul of a movement. And, while it's Anthony, Stanton, and Gage whose names are most prominently associated with it, the work speaks for countless women whose names might otherwise have been lost to history.

Isn't it remarkable what collaboration can achieve? What began as a conversation between friends became a seminal work charting the course of an entire movement. It's a testament to the fact that when strong, visionary women come together, history doesn't just get written; it gets rewritten.

Chapter 9

Turbulent Times: Controversies and Challenges

Picture a determined woman walking through a crowd, and eyes focused, steps sure, unwavering in her purpose. Susan B. Anthony wasn't just challenging societal norms but wading through a tumultuous sea of controversies and challenges. And yet, only some significant changes have its resistors.

America in the 19th century was a different world. Women, constrained by societal expectations and legal restrictions, were seldom seen beyond the confines of their homes. But Susan? She stood at the forefront, leading the charge for change. Why did she choose this challenging path? Perhaps because she believed, deep down, that the only way to shape the future was to confront the present.

One of the most defining moments in her life was her audacious act in 1872. Voting. Such a simple act, but for a woman? Revolutionary. When Susan cast her ballot, it wasn't just for a candidate. It was for every woman told her voice didn't matter. The result? She found herself under arrest. Shocking? Yes. But this act became a beacon, illuminating the suffrage movement's path.

Now, consider this: How do you counteract a society that refuses to hear you? Anthony's approach was simple yet brilliant. She took to the podium. Yet, every time she spoke, her words weren't just met with applause but often with open hostility. Eggs and rotten fruit were thrown her way, voices raised angrily, demanding silence. And through it all, she spoke. Wouldn't you wonder at times, as she must have, whether the trials were worth the outcome?

It wasn't just the public. Even within the suffrage movement, divisions arose. There were debates on strategy, methodology, and alliances. For instance, the 15th Amendment granted Black men the right to vote but left women, irrespective of race, on the sidelines. This posed a dilemma. Should the women's suffrage movement support an amendment that didn't include them? Susan believed in universal suffrage, but this topic's discord within the ranks was undeniable.

However, amidst this turbulence, Anthony's resolve was her compass. She fostered alliances, like her lifelong partnership with Elizabeth Cady Stanton. Together, they navigated the stormy waters of public opinion and internal disputes, always keeping the shore of their goal in sight. But what about those moments of solitude, those nights when the world's weight pressed down? Did she ever consider giving up?

The world around Susan B. Anthony was often hostile, challenging her at every turn. But here's the rub: Challenges often serve to clarify purpose. Controversies? They can highlight the very issues demanding attention. And for Susan, they became the stepping stones, not stumbling blocks, on her journey.

Reflecting on her life, it's essential to recognize that her path was far from smooth. It was laden with controversies, with challenges that tested her mettle. Yet, isn't that the true mark of a pioneer? To forge ahead, not because the path is easy, but because the destination is worth it. Anthony's journey, turbulent as it was, became the catalyst for change. And for that, history doesn't just remember her; it celebrates her.

Navigating Post-Civil War America

In the ashes of the Civil War, America stood divided. The land of the free, with its dream of equality, seemed miles from reaching its ideal. As the battle cries quieted and the nation began to heal its wounds, new challenges arose. Among them? The deep racial chasms persisted despite the abolition of slavery. Against this backdrop, where did Susan B. Anthony, our advocate for universal suffrage, fit in?

The tapestry of American society post-war was intricate and tumultuous. Black men were given the right to vote in 1870, thanks to the 15th Amendment. But what about Black women? And their white counterparts? These questions would give rise to some of the most defining moments in Susan's journey.

You see, Susan, at her core, believed in universal suffrage. This wasn't about gender or race for her but humanity. The idea is that every individual, irrespective of their background, deserves a say in the democratic process. However, the road to this ideal was fraught with difficult choices and compromises.

There were times, admittedly, when Anthony's methods faced scrutiny. Did she prioritize the suffrage of white women over Black individuals? These are the questions that historians still grapple with today. At the heart of this debate lies her collaboration with figures like Frederick Douglass, a formerly enslaved person and an ardent supporter of Black rights. Together, they stood united for the abolitionist cause in their younger years. But the post-war era, with its political complexities, strained this relationship.

While Douglass felt that Black men's suffrage was paramount in the immediate aftermath of the war, given their newfound freedom and the perils they faced, Anthony believed that sidelining women's voting rights was detrimental. This divergence in priorities, however, justified both stands and placed them on opposite ends of the spectrum.

One could argue: wasn't it natural for Douglass to prioritize Black men, given the violent racism they faced? And wasn't it understandable for Susan, after years of fighting for women's rights, to see this as another delay in achieving what she held so dear?

But beneath this surface-level conflict lay a deeper issue. The racial divide in America wasn't just about Black versus White; it was also interwoven with gender politics. Black women were at this complex intersection, navigating racial and gender prejudices.

Yet, despite these challenges, Anthony's legacy in the racial tapestry of America cannot be denied. Her fight was not just for white women or Black men alone but for an America where everyone's voice held weight. While still in the making, a dream began its journey in earnest with pioneers like her.

Susan B. Anthony's stand on racial issues remains contested in the annals of history. But as we sift through the pages of time, one thing becomes clear. In a divided America, striving for unity and understanding is the need of the hour. How will we apply the lessons from Susan's era to our own? The answer to that might shape the America of tomorrow.

State-by-State vs. Federal Amendments

In the crucible of any great movement, there's a moment – or many moments – where leaders must pause and ask: *What's our strategy?* For Susan B. Anthony and her contemporaries, this question wasn't simply about voting. It was about *how* to secure it. Dive deep into the annals of the women's rights movement, and one debate echoes loudly: Should they pursue a state-by-state strategy or aim directly for a federal amendment?

Imagine sitting in a dimly lit room, the air thick with tension. Anthony, her close collaborator Elizabeth Cady Stanton, and others grapple with this question. They knew the end goal: voting rights for women. But the road to get there? That was still under construction.

For some, the state-by-state approach seemed practical. By securing small victories one by one, they'd create momentum. Every state won would be another testament, another evidence to naysayers that change was not just necessary but inevitable. Lucy Stone, a vocal advocate for this strategy, believed that success in individual states could serve as a domino effect, setting the stage for broader change.

Yet for Anthony, the vision was clear: a federal amendment was the way forward. Why piecemeal progress when you can alter the Constitution itself and ensure rights for all women nationwide? Sure, it was ambitious. But isn't ambition the driver of change?

This debate wasn't merely theoretical; it dictated their every move. State-focused advocates would rally their troops in local legislatures, courting politicians, holding community gatherings, and pushing local news outlets to cover their cause. On the other hand, those like Anthony set their sights on the national stage, lobbying in Washington, garnering the attention of presidents, and ensuring the national conversation couldn't ignore women's suffrage.

But why did this distinction matter? Think of it this way: It's the difference between building a home brick by brick versus constructing an entire neighborhood at once. Both have merit but require different resources, strategies, and timelines.

As the years rolled on, the balance began to shift. The initial state-by-state victories, particularly in the West, gave the movement the momentum it desperately needed. However, these successes simultaneously showcased the limitations of a fragmented approach. With every state victory, there was a neighboring state with its heels dug in, resisting change.

By the early 20th century, the tide turned decisively toward the federal amendment strategy. Inspired by Anthony's vision, Alice Paul and Lucy Burns championed the cause, leading parades, organizing protests, and enduring force-feedings during hunger strikes. Their conviction was clear: Universal suffrage required a universal amendment.

So, while Anthony didn't live to see the day her dream was realized with the 19th Amendment in 1920, her strategic imprint was undeniable. Her unwavering belief in a federal solution shaped the movement's trajectory.

Ultimately, whether it was state-by-state or a sweeping federal amendment, the objective remained the same: to affirm that women, in every corner of the nation, had a voice that mattered. This strategic debate wasn't just about how to get there but ensuring that the change was here to stay once they did. The beauty of this movement? Even in debate, they never lost sight of the dream.

Introducing New Faces

Imagine a powerful and influential movement, yet always shifting, like sand beneath one's feet. Susan B. Anthony, a monumental figure in the women's suffrage movement, knew that for any endeavor to endure and evolve, new voices, fresh perspectives, and rejuvenated energies were essential. How did she usher in an era where leadership wasn't about a sole voice but an ensemble of spirited and passionate souls?

In the 19th century, the world was very different. Women in corsets, men in hats, and the idea of women voting? It's incredible to many. But not to Susan. She stood at the forefront, a beacon and a stalwart. However, this dynamo realized one thing early on: if the fight for women's rights were to cross generations, it needed more than just her at the helm.

Enter the new faces. A younger advocate, Carrie Chapman Catt, joined the suffrage chorus with an enthusiasm rivaling Susan's. Anthony saw potential there, didn't she? A new voice, a different method, but the same unwavering vision. Under Anthony's mentorship, Catt brought innovative strategies: well-coordinated campaigns and an emphasis on meticulous organization. The baton was passing.

And wasn't it captivating to watch Elizabeth Cady Stanton's daughter, Harriot Stanton Blatch, continue her mother's legacy but with her flavor? A breath of European socialist ideals and the fresh approach of mobilizing working women made her stand distinct. Harriot added another layer, another shade, to the movement's palette.

But let's pause for a moment: What does it mean to introduce new leadership? Was it just about bringing new faces to a podium? No. It was about evolution, which thrives on fresh perspectives while respecting foundational principles. Susan B. Anthony wasn't just creating space for new leaders but fostering an environment where diverse voices harmonized for a unified cause.

One can only discuss this evolving leadership with a nod to Alice Paul. Young, zealous, and radical. With her audacious methods, like the picketing of the White House, she made headlines. But she also made many listen. It was clear: the movement was no longer just a relic of the past but a pulsating, dynamic force echoing the sentiments of a younger generation.

Why does this evolution matter, you ask? Susan B. Anthony's foresight in integrating new voices ensured that the women's suffrage movement didn't remain static. It ebbed and flowed, adapted, and grew. Like a river that changes course but always reaches the sea, the movement, with its myriad of leaders, found its way.

And as we delve into the annals of history, isn't it remarkable to witness how the confluence of these unique voices, each shaping a different era, built a robust and resilient legacy? A legacy that began with Susan B. Anthony but was carried forward by the many she inspired. In the grand tapestry of women's suffrage, every thread, every color, every nuance counts. And so do the hands that wove them in.

Chapter 10

Towards the Nineteenth Amendment

The dawn of the 20th century: bustling cities, roaring engines, and jazz melodies wafting through the air. Yet, one fundamental right remained elusive for half the population: the right to vote. Susan B. Anthony, who had dedicated her life to this cause, was now old, with white hair and the lines of time on her face. But the fire in her eyes? That never wavered.

Imagine, for a moment, the sheer audacity of her vision. At a time when women were seen and not heard, Anthony envisioned a world where women stood shoulder to shoulder with men in the political arena. But how does one turn such dreams into reality?

Step by step, with each setback only fueling the resolve. Meetings in dimly lit parlors, fervent letters passed between hands, impassioned speeches that captured the public's attention: the movement grew. At its heart was Susan, but she wasn't alone. The suffrage movement was a symphony of voices, each contributing its unique note.

Elizabeth Cady Stanton was the philosopher, wasn't she? With her knack for framing arguments, she laid the theoretical groundwork. Anthony and Stanton were an unstoppable duo: one providing the intellectual might, the other the relentless drive. Theirs was a collaboration of heart and mind, forging the path for generations of women.

But the journey wasn't without its obstacles. The establishment pushed back, society scoffed, and even allies sometimes disagreed. Remember the discord between the National Woman Suffrage Association and the American Woman Suffrage Association? Factions differing views, but the ultimate goal was singular. Unification became inevitable as the National American Woman Suffrage Association emerged, consolidating the drive toward the vote.

As the years rolled on, new players entered the scene. Think of Alice Paul, with her youth and zeal, staging protests and courting arrest. Or Carrie Chapman Catt, with her strategic genius, ensured the movement never lost momentum. Anthony recognized the need for these fresh voices, understanding that the torch must be passed and carried forward.

And then, 1920 arrived. The dream was also realized in an era of the flappers dancing and literature blossoming. The Nineteenth Amendment to the U.S. Constitution was ratified! It was a moment of triumph for Susan B. Anthony and every woman who dared to dream alongside her. It must have been poignant for those who remembered Anthony's words, "Failure is impossible."

While Anthony wasn't there to cast her ballot, her spirit undoubtedly permeated every polling station. Young and older women stepping up to have their say bore testament to her legacy. The Nineteenth Amendment wasn't just a piece of legislation; it was a dream realized, a testament to decades of struggle, passion, and collaboration.

It prompts us to ponder: What takes turning a dream into reality? Grit, vision, teamwork, and the unwavering belief that change is not just possible but inevitable. As we reflect on the journey towards the Nineteenth Amendment, we remember Susan B. Anthony and the myriad voices that echoed her call, culminating in a chorus that changed the course of history.

Reflecting on a Life's Mission

In the twilight of her years, as the 20th century was dawning, Susan B. Anthony might have often found herself in the quiet sanctum of her thoughts, reflecting. Did she ever imagine, when she began, the monumental impact she would leave behind? What dreams still flitted in her aging eyes as she pondered her life's mission?

Rochester, New York, the place she called home for much of her life, bore witness to many of her introspections. The creaky floors of her house whispered tales of countless meetings, passionate debates, and dreams of a future where women were equals. It was a space where the fragrance of old papers - letters, petitions, drafts of speeches - mingled with the aroma of brewed tea.

And those letters! They must have transported her to moments of great challenge and greater triumph. Correspondences with Elizabeth Cady Stanton, her longtime collaborator and friend, perhaps elicited a smile or a tear. Together, they had taken on a world that wasn't always kind to audacious dreamers like them. Like the intertwining branches of two stalwart trees, their partnership was one for the ages. But what did Susan think of their journey?

She probably remembered the criticism, the ridicule. Times when society seemed an insurmountable fortress, its gates firmly shut against them. Did doubts ever plague her? If they did, they certainly didn't deter her. For Susan's spirit was not one to be cowed. The hardships, in fact, only steeled her resolve.

Yet, the Susan of these final years wasn't just a beacon of the past. She keenly felt the winds of change. The new century brought fresh voices and renewed vigor to the suffrage movement. Inspired by her foundation, young women were carrying the torch forward. They marched, they protested, they demanded. And Anthony? She watched, perhaps with a mix of pride and anticipation.

It's said that the mark of true leaders is the legacy they leave behind. They plant seeds not necessarily to enjoy the shade of the trees but to ensure that future generations reap the benefits. And Susan B. Anthony, in her final years, must have felt the stirrings of that legacy.

She remarked, "I think the girl who can earn her living and pay her way should be as happy as anybody on Earth." These weren't just words for her. They embodied her lifelong mission: to pave the way for women to claim their rightful place in society.

In 1906, when Susan B. Anthony bid the world farewell, she left behind memories and a movement on the brink of monumental success. While she didn't live to witness the ratification of the Nineteenth Amendment, her spirit undoubtedly soared with every woman who walked into the voting booth.

Reflecting on her final years, we are reminded that while life's journey is finite, the dreams we foster and the change we champion can ripple through eternity. And Susan's ripples? They turned into mighty waves, reshaping the course of history — a fitting reflection on a life's mission.

Who Took Up the Cause

Imagine a world not bound by the silencing restrictions of gender, where one's voice isn't subdued because they're a woman. Sounds ideal. Well, Susan B. Anthony tirelessly dreamed of such a world. Yet, in her wake, she wasn't the lone soldier in this battle. Many picked up the banner she so courageously raised, carrying forth the burning embers of her revolution. So who were these torchbearers?

Stepping out of the shadow of the 19th century, a brigade of women, fierce and determined, stepped up. Elizabeth Cady Stanton was one such force. Her friendship and collaboration with Susan was legendary. Together, they formed a formidable duo, penning passionate speeches and rallying countless to their cause. Their bond went beyond shared beliefs; it was a profound connection, an intertwining of souls set ablaze by a shared purpose. It's said that friendships carve paths, and theirs carved a highway toward equality.

Then there was Lucy Stone. Though sometimes at odds with Susan's methods, Stone had a similar vision. Founder of the Woman's Journal, a publication advocating women's rights, Stone's voice resonated in print and on the podium. Isn't it curious how the same goal can be approached from different angles, yet the heart remains united?

But the march didn't halt there. Ida B. Wells, a force in her own right, expanded the battlefront. Not only did she champion women's suffrage, but she also bravely confronted the horrors of racial discrimination. It's daunting to juggle two colossal fights, but Wells was no ordinary woman. With every article she wrote and every speech she delivered, she reminded the world that the fight for gender equality is intertwined with the battle against racial injustice.

Carrie Chapman Catt was another luminary who navigated the terrain shaped by Anthony. Succeeding Anthony as the National American Woman Suffrage Association president, Catt introduced new strategies to lobby Congress, and momentum surged under her leadership. It's a marvel how one person's dedication can rejuvenate an entire movement.

And let's remember Alice Paul. Younger than the rest, she brought a renewed energy, employing dramatic means like hunger strikes to draw attention. In the grand tapestry of the suffrage movement, Paul's thread was vibrant and impossible to ignore.

So, why do these names matter? Why is it crucial to know who took up the mantle of Susan B. Anthony?

Because movements, like rivers, flow beyond their origin. They twist, turn, expand, and touch new shores. While Susan was a monumental source, the river of women's rights was fed by many tributaries, each bringing its richness.

It's a heartening realization: the flame Susan B. Anthony kindled didn't flicker out with her. It was passed on, hand to hand, heart to heart. And these torchbearers? They ensured it became an inferno, an unstoppable force that roared through history.

The journey toward equality wasn't walked alone. It was a dance of many feet, a chorus of many voices. And while Susan led the charge, she was joined by a legion, each echoing the same powerful sentiment: onward until every chain is broken — quite a vision.

Celebrating the Victory

The journey to freedom often has its share of battles, each victory sweetened by the sweat and tears of its champions. And what can be a sweeter victory than the ratification of the Nineteenth Amendment? An event that not only marked a significant milestone in the tapestry of American history but was also a testament to the indomitable spirit of women like Susan B. Anthony.

Have you ever paused and tried to feel the pulse of a moment? Picture this: The year is 1920. America stands at the threshold of a new era. Newsboys shout at street corners, their papers announcing the triumphant ratification. Women across the nation, young and old, can now hear the resonating beats of change. An arduous journey that began decades earlier was culminating in this crowning moment.

What fueled this monumental change? Let's step back a bit. Susan B. Anthony, with her cadre of fierce suffragettes, embarked on a relentless crusade. They marched, protested, and even faced imprisonment. Their grit became the bedrock upon which this constitutional change rested. While Susan couldn't cast her vote legally, the winds of change she stirred couldn't be contained.

Elizabeth Cady Stanton, Anthony's lifelong comrade in arms, once penned, "The best protection any woman can have... is courage." And courage they had in abundance! Their tenacity and their undying spirit became infectious. State after state began to recognize the right of women to vote. Momentum built up, wave after powerful wave, until the tide was simply undeniable.

The day the Amendment got the green light, a hush fell upon the suffrage headquarters in Nashville, Tennessee. Can you imagine the raw emotion in that room? The triumph? The payback? Jubilant cheers echoed across the hallways when the news broke, reverberating with decades of struggle and passion. The suffragettes, those indomitable spirits, had finally etched their mark on the Constitution!

But what about the Nineteenth Amendment made it such a landmark? Simply put, it bridged a chasm. Before its ratification, democracy in America was, in essence, half-represented. Half the voices were subdued. But post-ratification? The symphony of democracy grew louder, richer, and more inclusive.

However, it wasn't just a win on paper. The aftermath was palpable. Women, invigorated by their newly acquired rights, began to assert themselves in various spheres. Politics, academia, the arts: you name it! Their perspectives began to reshape the nation's narrative, lending it nuances previously overlooked.

And Susan B. Anthony? Though she didn't live to see this day, her legacy was there in every ballot drop, every tick on a voting slip. For every woman who walked into a polling booth, a piece of Susan's dream was realized.

So, the next time you pass by a voting station or glimpse a campaign poster, pause for a moment. Behind that simple act of casting a vote lies a saga of determination, a story of relentless pursuit. And at the heart of it? Women like Susan B. Anthony, who dared to dream, dared to challenge, and dared to change the course of history — quite a legacy.

Chapter 11

Remembering Susan: Tributes and Monuments

Imagine walking through a serene park, the trees softly rustling, the sun casting mellow hues. Amidst the symphony of nature, a statue stands tall, resonating strength and defiance. You draw closer, and the features become familiar. That determined gaze, that poised stance: it's Susan B. Anthony.

But why is this legendary suffragette immortalized in stone, metal, and even our memories? What draws thousands to these monuments, year after year, to pay tribute?

Susan's life wasn't just a tale of personal ambition. Her journey was an embodiment of a collective aspiration: equality. Across America, in parks, squares, and university campuses, reminders of her undying spirit stand. But these aren't just cold, lifeless statues. They're beacons of inspiration, urging future generations to keep pushing the boundaries.

In Rochester, New York, a particular gravesite witnesses an unusual spectacle every election day. Here, people line up not to mourn but to celebrate. They place their "I Voted" stickers upon Susan B. Anthony's gravestone, transforming it into a mosaic of gratitude. Isn't it symbolic? The right she fought for is being exercised by many, regardless of gender, and they converge here, at her resting place, in acknowledgment.

Another iconic tribute stands in the U.S. Capitol's Rotunda. Susan has been cast in bronze with her long-time collaborator and friend, Elizabeth Cady Stanton, and fellow suffragette Lucretia Mott. The tableau speaks volumes. Three indomitable women, forever frozen in time, yet their ideals and convictions remain as fluid and influential as ever.

Have you ever visited the Susan B. Anthony Museum and House in Rochester? Walking through those corridors feels like a journey back in time. Every artifact and photograph whispers tales of her tireless advocacy for women's rights. Visitors often remark they can almost hear the echoes of her speeches, feel the weight of her determination, and sense the magnetism of her personality.

How about the countless portraits, sketches, and photographs? They're not just reminiscent of her physical likeness but are imbued with the essence of her character. Don't they feel respect when someone gazes upon these portraits? I admired a woman who stared adversity in the face and said, "I will not be moved."

The 19th Amendment, which granted women the right to vote, is the most fitting tribute to her life's work. Though she never got to cast a vote legally in her lifetime, every ballot cast by a woman in America is a silent nod to her relentless efforts.

Monuments and tributes aside, Susan B. Anthony's greatest legacy might be the ripple effect of her actions. Every debate she ignited, rally she organized, and her speech set a wave of change in motion. Today, countless women leaders, activists, and thinkers stand on her shoulders, drawing inspiration and strength.

In the end, isn't that what true tribute is all about? Not just chiseling a name into stone but engraving an ideology into the very fabric of society. The statues will weather, and photographs will fade, but the monumental impact Susan B. Anthony had on civil rights? That's an eternal flame, illuminating pathways for generations yet unborn. Quite a legacy, wouldn't you agree?

Her Passing and Public Mourning

If ever there was a woman who seemed larger than life, it was Susan B. Anthony. Her enthusiasm with which she championed women's rights, her sacrifices, and the challenges she faced head-on gave her an aura of invincibility. So, when news broke on that fateful day in March 1906 of her passing, the nation was left reeling.

Who could have imagined a world without Susan's fiery speeches, undaunted spirit, or tireless advocacy? Isn't it often said that certain souls are so vibrant and impactful that their absence feels almost... surreal?

Across America, grief hung thick in the air. Cities, big and small, mourned the loss of a woman who wasn't just a national figure but a personal beacon of hope for so many. Flags flew at half-mast, church bells tolled, and an unspoken sorrow bound communities together.

Newspapers the next day painted a poignant picture. Headlines weren't just clinical announcements of her demise; they felt more like heart-wrenching eulogies. "Susan B. Anthony: Beacon of Hope Extinguished!" one read. Another declared, "The Nation Loses its Guiding Star!". With each line, readers could sense the weight of the loss, the void left by a colossus in the fight for equal rights.

Across households, stories of Susan were shared: tales of her early days, her dogged pursuits, her clashes with naysayers, and the indomitable spirit that defined her. Parents whispered to their children, "Remember Susan. Be like Susan." A call to arms to keep her legacy alive in young, impressionable minds.

Public figures, from politicians to poets, felt the need to vocalize their grief. Elizabeth Cady Stanton, Anthony's stalwart ally and friend, said of her: "In her loyalty, sincerity, and incorruptible integrity, she was akin to the saints." Beautiful words, capturing the essence of a life well-lived, a battle bravely fought.

But amidst the sea of sorrow, a palpable determination emerged. The public mourning wasn't just about paying respects. It became an avenue to remember what Susan fought for, to ensure her dream wasn't buried with her. An undercurrent of resilience surged through the nation: her mission would continue.

Communities began to rally together, organizing memorials, discussions, and gatherings. They reminisced about Susan, but, more importantly, they talked about the future. How could they take her work forward? What could they do to ensure her dream of gender equality became a palpable reality?

Public spaces became arenas of tribute. Parks, squares, and auditoriums echoed her words and her beliefs. Spontaneous gatherings saw men and women talking, debating, and pledging. It wasn't just about mourning a loss but celebrating a legacy. And what a legacy it was!

So, while Susan B. Anthony might have physically left the world, her essence remained stronger than ever. The public mourning wasn't an end but a beautiful beginning: a renewed commitment to a dream, a pledge to carry the torch she once held so high.

In the years that followed, as women finally secured the right to vote and other significant victories, one thing became evident: Susan's spirit was indomitable. Through public mourning and memories, she had achieved something truly incredible: a form of immortality. Not just in statues or books, but in ideals and dreams, in every ballot cast by a woman, and in the heart of a nation she forever changed. What more could one ask for after a life so fiercely lived?

Monuments in Her Honor

Think for a moment: how do societies choose to commemorate those who've marked the annals of history with their indelible spirit? Often, it is through monuments. Hulking bronze and stone, these structures are everlasting reminders of legacies that refuse to fade. Such monuments seem fitting for

Susan B. Anthony, a formidable, strength, and conviction woman.

In bustling cities and quiet towns across America, you might stumble upon a statue of a determined woman with a fixed gaze on the horizon. Susan. These aren't just decorative installations. They're a testament to a woman who, in a time dominated by men, declared with unwavering certainty: "Failure is impossible."

The very first time a Susan B. Anthony monument graced public spaces, there was an electric air of anticipation. People flocked from miles away, brimming with excitement, pride, and perhaps a touch of nostalgia. It wasn't just about seeing a piece of art but about rekindling memories of a woman who dared to challenge the status quo.

A remarkable bronze statue stands in Rochester, New York, the heart of Susan's activism. Susan stands alongside her close collaborator, Elizabeth Cady Stanton, and Sojourner Truth - three women's rights movement stalwarts. Isn't it poetic? Three women, unified in purpose, immortalized in bronze.

These statues, while mute, seem to whisper tales of Susan's audacious life. The challenges she faced, the skeptics she proved wrong, the relentless energy with which she pursued justice. Each curve and each line on the statue captures an essence of her, drawing visitors into her world, her struggles, and her triumphs.

But the reactions they elicit are more heartening than the statues themselves. Parents are hoisting children on their shoulders, pointing at the statue, weaving tales of a time when women couldn't vote. The spark in the young eyes, the murmurs of "I want to be like her," the sense of reverence in the air. These monuments, in ways more than one, bridge generations.

As the sun sets, casting long shadows of these stone and bronze monoliths, one can't help but marvel. Isn't it incredible how Susan B. Anthony continues to inspire decades after her passing? These statues are not just cold, inanimate structures. They're living, breathing, embodying her spirit, courage, and unwavering commitment.

A Washington, D.C. park has a bench with a simple plaque dedicated to Susan. It invites visitors to sit, reflect, and converse with the spirit of Susan. Imagine that: a quiet conversation under a canopy of trees with one of history's fiercest advocates for equality.

So, the next time you're wandering through a city or town and chance upon a monument of Susan B. Anthony, pause for a moment. Please think of the battles she fought, the society she transformed, and the legacy she left behind. And as you walk away, remember: these monuments aren't just about the past. They're beacons, guiding the future, urging us to carry forward the torch Susan once held so high. After all, as she taught us, the journey for true equality is never truly over.

Museums, Houses, and Celebrations

When you walk the cobbled streets of historic American towns, can you feel the echoes of the past? It was a time of tumult, revolution, and unwavering determination. Among those memories, Susan B. Anthony's spirit is palpable.

Imagine standing at the threshold of Susan's family home. The wooden panels, the faded paint, the timeworn steps leading to the entrance. Each corner of that house, nestled in Adams, Massachusetts, carries tales of a family that believed in social justice long before it became a rallying cry. Can you almost hear the lively debates that once filled the rooms, the earnest discussions on abolition and temperance?

And it's not just the house. Museums across the country chronicle her life with a finesse that's both engaging and enlightening. Artifacts, letters, photographs: glimpses into a woman's life who repeatedly proved that one individual could shake the foundations of an entire nation. Delve into these archives, and there's a revelation at every turn. Did you know, for instance, about the countless hours she spent penning letters to rally support for women's suffrage? The meticulous planning behind each campaign, each speech, each protest? These museums don't just display relics; they breathe life into history.

Now, picture this. Crowds gather yearly in Rochester, New York, to celebrate Susan B. Anthony Day. The enthusiasm, the spirit of unity, it's almost infectious. People of all ages and backgrounds come together, united by their admiration for a woman who refused to let societal norms dictate her destiny.

Young children recite her speeches, their voices ringing with clarity and conviction. Artists display paintings, sculptures, and sketches, each capturing a different facet of Susan's multifaceted personality. There's music, dance, and an unbridled celebration of a legacy that remains unmatched.

And amidst all this stands the Susan B. Anthony Museum & House. More than just a building, it's a monument to her tireless efforts. It's where she was arrested for daring to vote, where she strategized with fellow activists, where she penned some of her most impactful speeches. Every room has a story, every artifact a piece of a puzzle that shaped the America we know today. As you walk its corridors, there's a sense of reverence, a realization of the sheer magnitude of her contributions.

But why, you might ask, is this emphasis on museums, houses, and celebrations? Because they serve as tangible connections to the past. They remind us that history isn't just a series of dates and events. It's about people—real, flesh-and-blood individuals who, with their courage and tenacity, forged the path for future generations.

These establishments and events aren't just about looking back and moving forward. They inspire, they educate, they challenge. They pose a simple question: If Susan B. Anthony could achieve so much in her time, what's stopping us from doing the same in ours?

So the next time you find yourself in a museum dedicated to her or celebrating her legacy in some corner of the country, take a moment. Absorb the history, feel the weight of her achievements, and carry that inspiration with you. After all, as Susan herself believed: "The day may be approaching when the whole world will recognize woman as the equal of man." And with every museum visit, every celebration, every reminder of her legacy, we inch closer to that day.

Chapter 12

Legacy Echoes: Anthony's Lasting Impact

Has there ever been a time when a name invoked such passion, determination, and relentless pursuit of justice? Susan B. Anthony's legacy is not one of mere memory but a living, breathing force that still shapes our world today. But what about this woman still resonates so deeply with us?

The late 19th century was a tumultuous time, defined by social upheavals, technological innovations, and challenges to the very fabric of societal norms. Enter Susan. She was born into a Quaker family that valued education and believed in equality, so her destiny seemed preordained. Yet, it was her own fierce conviction and unyielding spirit that propelled her into the limelight.

Remember the time when women were seen but seldom heard? Anthony questioned: why should that be the norm? With every speech, every rally, and every petition, she dismantled the patriarchal beliefs that sought to muzzle women's voices. And, in doing so, she did not stand alone. Collaborating with like-minded powerhouses like Elizabeth Cady Stanton, the duo formed an unbeatable team, challenging conventions and demanding justice.

However, her fight wasn't limited to voting alone. Whether advocating for equal pay or challenging laws denying women property rights, Anthony stood as a beacon of hope. A beacon that whispered, "Change is possible."

Today, we live in a world transformed by her efforts. The ripples of her actions can be seen in the ballot boxes, where women cast their votes with pride; in boardrooms, where female leaders make groundbreaking decisions; and in homes, where girls grow up knowing they can aspire to any dream.

Yet, have we truly realized the world she envisioned? The fact that her struggle is still referenced suggests there's work to be done. Indeed, while many battles have been won, the war for total equality continues.

Visit any institution of learning, and her name adorns the walls. Scholars and students alike delve into her writings, speeches, and actions, drawing inspiration for their pursuits. As they navigate the historical accounts, there's a realization: Susan B. Anthony's journey wasn't just about the destination – it was about igniting a spark that would outlive her. And, boy, did it!

When you attend women's marches, hear of legislation passed in favor of women's rights, or witness young girls speak confidently about their aspirations, think: isn't Anthony's spirit still very much alive? Each step forward, each milestone achieved, is a testament to her life's work. A nod to a woman who refused to be silenced.

As the sun sets on another day, somewhere, a young girl reads about Susan B. Anthony, her eyes widening with amazement. The stories of marches, arrests, and unwavering spirit fill her with a sense of purpose. And as she dreams of the future, Anthony's legacy echoes, reassuring her that the world is her oyster and she should claim it. Because if history has taught us anything, it's that voices like Anthony's – once raised – never truly fade. They linger, they inspire, and most importantly, they drive change. What will you do with the legacy she's left behind?

Feminism's First Wave

In a time when women were largely confined to the roles society dictated, a powerful force emerged from the shadows: Susan B. Anthony. How did a woman from a Quaker family in Massachusetts become one of the pillars of the first wave of feminism? Let's take a journey.

Susan B. Anthony wasn't merely born into the activist world; it coursed through her veins. Her early years, rooted in a Quaker upbringing, whispered the early ideals of equality and justice. Did it surprise anyone that she'd soon stand up to the tide and challenge the status quo?

Picture this: It's mid-19th century America. While the country thrives on the principles of liberty, half of its population remains shackled, not by chains, but by societal norms and legal restrictions. Susan, with her passion and unwavering commitment, recognized this disparity. And it wasn't something she'd let slide.

In her travels, Anthony crossed paths with Elizabeth Cady Stanton. What followed was not just a friendship but a partnership that would rock the foundations of American society. Stanton, with her flair for writing, and Anthony, with her unparalleled knack for organizing, became the dynamic duo the feminist movement needed. But what drove Anthony's passion?

For Susan, the suffrage movement wasn't merely about giving women a voice in politics. It encompassed much more: a woman's right to her own property, her choice in marriage, her decisions about her own body, and yes, her voice in the very foundation of democracy - voting. Why should women be spectators in a play where they should rightfully be actors?

Together with Stanton, Anthony founded the American Equal Rights Association in 1866. But it's worth noting that their collaboration could have been better. The duo faced numerous setbacks, societal ridicule, legal trials, and the sheer frustration of slow progress. Yet, Anthony's dedication never wavered. Was it her ironclad belief in the cause or the sea of women who looked up to her for direction? A mix of both could be possible.

One of the defining moments of Anthony's activism was her audacious act of casting a vote in the 1872 presidential election. An act deemed illegal for women at the time. And while she was fined, this bold move spotlighted the glaring inconsistencies in American democracy. Can a nation that prides itself on freedom and equality deny half its populace a basic right?

Anthony's influence permeated deeper than just political rights. She made ripples in spheres like education, championing coeducation and women's entry into traditionally male-dominated fields. Moreover, her stand against the restrictive women's attire of the time pushed forward a revolution in fashion, leading to the adoption of the more practical bloomer costume. Isn't it fascinating how her influence wasn't just monumental and multifaceted?

The first wave of feminism, focusing on legal rights and suffrage, found in Susan B. Anthony, a leader, a visionary, and most importantly, an embodiment of the change it sought. While she didn't live to see the ratification of the 19th Amendment granting women the right to vote, it stands as a testament to her relentless efforts.

Susan B. Anthony's life and work are not just tales from a history book but reminders. Reminders of the battles fought, the adversities overcome, and the distance we've come in the fight for equality. And as we forge ahead, her legacy remains, illuminating our path: a beacon of hope, resilience, and unwavering commitment.

Continuing the Figh

Imagine, for a moment, a world where the echoes of the past blend seamlessly with the voices of the present. The activism landscape we witness today, charged with vigor and passion, hasn't sprung out of a vacuum. Instead, its roots trace back to trailblazers like Susan B. Anthony. Do you ever wonder how the ripples of her activism resonate in the modern movements of today?

Susan B. Anthony, a name synonymous with unwavering resolve, challenged societal norms and the very fabric of American democracy. From casting that audacious vote in 1872 to rallying cries for women's rights, her legacy is felt even today. But how do the battles she fought and her steps mirror our contemporary world?

The modern feminist wave, a tide teeming with fierce advocates for gender equality, draws inspiration from the foundational work of Susan and her peers. Isn't it astonishing that the grit and determination of one woman in the 19th century can inspire millions today? Anthony's belief in equal rights, whether in voting, education, or employment, finds resonance in the 21st-century fight against wage disparity, reproductive rights, and the glass ceiling. Yet, while we've made strides, have we also recognized that the journey is far from over?

Our era has witnessed the birth and growth of movements like #MeToo, a collective outcry against sexual harassment. When activists take to the streets, platforms, and courts today, a closer listen reveals a faint whisper: a nod to Anthony's unwavering spirit. Her battles might have been different, but the core essence? A thirst for justice, a dream of equality. And that's universal.

Black Lives Matter, a movement for the rights and dignity of Black individuals, parallels Anthony's tenets of universal suffrage and equality while distinct in its focus. While Susan predominantly advocated for women, her ethos transcends gender: everyone, regardless of race, gender, or creed, deserves respect and equal rights. Isn't that the very backbone of the democracy we so cherish?

With its tweets, hashtags, and viral campaigns, the digital age might seem worlds apart from Susan's era of pamphlets and town hall speeches. Yet, the spirit remains unchanged. Today's activists, armed with social media and global platforms, amplify their voices just as Anthony did with her speeches and publications. The mediums have evolved, but the heartbeat of the message? It beats just as strong.

What's truly awe-inspiring is how Susan's legacy isn't confined to women's rights. LGBTQ+ rights, a pivotal focus of the modern age, find an ally in Susan's foundational beliefs. While she might not have explicitly championed this cause in her time, her overarching vision of equality and justice for all resonates deeply with the movement's ethos.

In wrapping our journey through the corridors of the present, touched by the echoes of the past, one realization stands out: the essence of Susan B. Anthony's life and work isn't a chapter that we close and move on from. It's a continuous narrative, shaping and being shaped by the world, even today. As we look ahead, with challenges old and new, don't we often find strength in the echoes of Susan's timeless spirit?

Inspiring Generations

Imagine walking on a crowded street in the 21st century and then catching a glimpse of a familiar face from the pages of history. Would it surprise you if that face was Susan B. Anthony's? It shouldn't. While deeply rooted in the 19th century, Anthony's influence finds numerous echoes in the heart of our contemporary culture.

Stepping into the 1800s, Susan B. Anthony was more than just an activist; she was a storm of change. From challenging the oppressive barriers placed on women to pioneering the right for them to vote, Susan reshaped the contours of society. But what happens when history melds with the present? How does a 19th-century firebrand affect today's hashtags, conversations, and ethos?

One can argue that the sheer volume of conversations surrounding women's rights and gender equality might not have existed without Susan's relentless efforts. Dive into the world of film and literature; her presence is unmistakable. Movies portraying strong women taking charge of their destinies, books delving into feminist theories, and art installations celebrating women's achievements – don't they all owe a bit to Anthony's pioneering spirit?

Have you ever attended a women's rights rally or witnessed a sea of pink hats during the Women's March? Behind the myriad of placards and fervent slogans, a sentiment can be traced back to Susan. She might not have had social media, but if she did, wouldn't her tweets be the kind that sparks revolutions?

Yet, her influence isn't restricted merely to feminist arenas. Susan B. Anthony became an emblem for all those who felt voiceless, marginalized and suppressed. Across various social movements today, whether championing LGBTQ+ rights or advocating racial equality, isn't there a piece of Susan's spirit urging everyone on? Every time an individual stands up against injustice, somewhere in the fabric of their courage, there are threads spun by Anthony.

In its myriad forms, popular culture is teeming with references to Susan. Take currency, for instance. Remember the excitement surrounding the announcement that Anthony would grace the $1 coin? That's not just metal and mint. It's an acknowledgment, a hat tip to a woman who altered the course of history.

Now, think about the classrooms. Children today learn about Susan B. Anthony as a historical figure and a symbol of resistance, resilience, and reform. Using her tales, teachers inspire young minds to question, challenge, and never accept the status quo. How empowering is that?

In a world swamped by fleeting trends and ephemeral influences, Susan's impact stands tall, undiminished by time. From a young girl questioning gender norms to a writer penning a narrative on social justice, from a politician drafting policies to an artist sketching a portrait of change, they carry a fragment of Anthony in their hearts and minds.

Ultimately, it's essential to ask: would today's culture be as vibrant, challenging, and transformative without the lessons imbibed from Susan B. Anthony? Maybe, but it sure would lack the depth, the legacy, and the echoes of a woman who, centuries ago, decided that change was not just a dream but a mission.

Literature and Resources

When diving deep into the life of Susan B. Anthony, it's a journey filled with determination, challenges, and pivotal moments that shaped not only her existence but the very fabric of American society. It's only possible to capture her essence by referencing foundational sources that offer glimpses into her world. Below are some resources that served as touchstones while crafting this biography.

1. Books: Harper, Ida Husted. "Life and Work of Susan B. Anthony." This extensive biography is often considered the most detailed account of Susan B. Anthony's life, spread across multiple volumes.
Griffith, Elisabeth. "In Her Own Right: The Life of Susan B. Anthony." An interpretative biography that paints a vivid picture of the woman behind the movement.

2. Archives and Collections: Susan B. Anthony Papers, Library of Congress, Washington D.C.: A treasure trove of letters, diaries, and documents that provide intimate details of Anthony's life.
The National Susan B. Anthony Museum & House, Rochester, New York: An establishment preserving Anthony's home and offering a wealth of knowledge about her legacy and the suffrage movement.

3. Websites:

[The Susan B. Anthony Center]: Established by the University of Rochester, this center aims to advance the legacy of its namesake by promoting issues she values.

[Women of the Hall]: The National Women's Hall of Fame initiative offers details on Susan B. Anthony's induction and her contributions.

4. Articles:

"The Trial of Susan B. Anthony for Illegal Voting," *American Heritage* Magazine, 1953. This piece delves into the specifics of her 1873 trial.

"Susan B. Anthony: The Early Years," *Smithsonian Magazine*, 2010. An enlightening exploration of Anthony's younger years and the seeds of her activism.

5. Lectures and Talks:

Stanton, Elizabeth Cady. "The Friendship of Elizabeth Cady Stanton and Susan B. Anthony," delivered at various suffrage meetings. This talk offers insight into the bond between two iconic figures of the suffrage movement.

6. Primary Sources:

Anthony, Susan B. "Declaration of Rights of the Women of the United States." Presented in 1876, this text showcases Anthony's persuasive eloquence and her vision for women's rights.

In crafting a narrative around the monumental life of Susan B. Anthony, the reliance on authentic, reputable sources is essential. These references serve as guideposts, ensuring accuracy while allowing the rich tapestry of her life to unfold in all its authenticity and grandeur. The above resources are just a glimpse into the extensive material available on this revolutionary figure. Exploring them would be an enlightening experience for anyone seeking to delve deeper into the world of Susan B. Anthony.